successful small groups

from concept to practice

teena m. stewart

BEACON HILL PRESS
OF KANSAS CITY

Library of Congress Cataloging-in-Publication Data

Stewart, Teena.
    Successful small groups : from concept to practice / Teena M. Stewart.
        p. cm.
    Includes bibliographical references.
    ISBN 978-0-8341-2337-3 (pbk.)
    1. Church group work. 2. Small groups. I. Title.

    BV652.2.S74 2007
    253'.7—dc22

                                                                    2007044067

10 9 8 7 6 5 4 3 2 1

contents

introduction

My varied experience as a pastor's wife, ministry team leader, spiritual gifts seminar teacher, small-group leader, and editor of a ministry-related Web resource keeps me right in the heart of church ministry. Experience is a great teacher (if not a painful one), and this is true not only in the family but also in the church family.

Parents give their children advice to spare them future heartaches and headaches. As a Christian ministry facilitator I feel a parental responsibility toward others in ministry. Like my husband, Jeff, who oversees discipleship and small groups at our church, I see parallels to parenting that relate to small groups.

Every group has its own unique personality—just as children do—and must be managed according to its makeup. As a small-group leader, you cannot always take a blanket approach but must adapt to meet the personality. My desire is to communicate what I know about small-group ministry to make your job as leader and/or small-group ministry developer as headache and heartache free as possible.

I've had many opportunities to participate in and lead small groups, and I want to pass on what I learned from churches and small-group leaders. With that in mind, this book is for novice small-group leaders, experienced group leaders, and those helping to launch and facilitate small groups.

Every church is different and has its own size, style, and culture. Groups reflect their church's ministry purpose, focus, and way of operating. A church's size and focus dictates how many small groups are established within that church and how it manages them.

Keeping a flexible attitude, adjusting content to suit your particular church and groups while adapting it for small-group leader training workshops, may also prove beneficial. Included at the end of each chapter is a Points to Ponder section designed to help you consider effective ways to manage groups and determine potential work areas.

Small groups radically change the lives of those who participate in them. Rather than feeling isolated and forgotten, members feel a sense of belonging to a caring community. Groups provide not only a safe haven for believers but also an environment of encouragement and exhortation spurring them to press on toward the goal as they work toward maturity.

My prayer is that this book will help you help others as we bring them to Christian maturity through successful small-group fellowship.

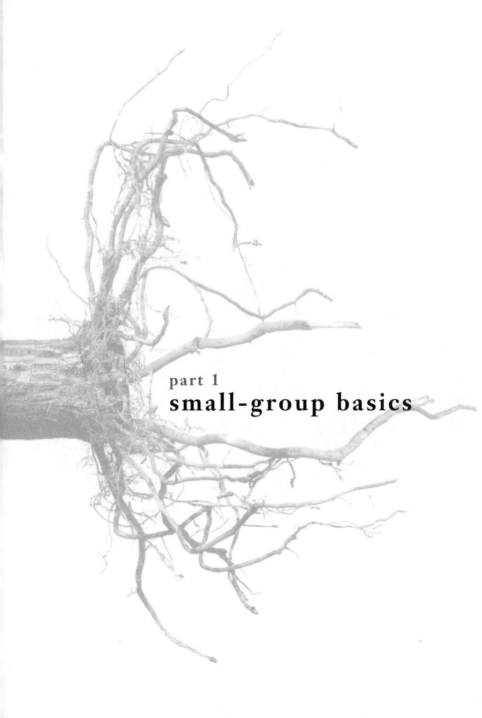

part 1
small-group basics

Bible Study
Joyce Meyer
Service -
Oath / Agreement
Snack
Needs of each other
Service
Love one another
Journaling
Prayer

1 small groups—big impact

> There are two things you cannot do alone:
> marry and be a Christian.
> —Paul Tournier[1]

Ask a leader of a growing and thriving church why the church is growing and thriving and he or she will likely tell you that small groups are a major reason. I have been involved in Christian small groups for many years and have seen firsthand the life transformation they bring about. Small groups secure a strong foundation for those wanting to experience the fullness of Christian community and grow mature in Christ.

Though many churches use the term *small groups* to refer to them, in reality small groups are known by a diversity of labels. You might hear them dubbed cell groups, Bible study groups, fellowship groups, affinity groups, recovery groups, core groups, community groups, branch groups, home-life groups, support groups, or even care groups.

Many more names abound. Despite the myriad of names, most Christian small groups have several features in common. They provide a sense of community and support for church members while giving them a safe and enjoyable atmosphere where they can learn biblical principles and grow in spiritual maturity together as a family.

More and more churches are developing effective small-group ministries because they realize such groups are crucial for a healthy church ministry and for the maturation of the Christians they serve.

Key to Kingdom Building

A crucial part of church planting includes learning as much as possible about the community in which you plan to build. A church planter and his wife establishing a church in a small northern California town canvassed residents in a door-to-door survey. Their interview included questions about lifestyle and culture and revealed a prominent felt need. Despite being surrounded by neighbors in a highly populated area, many people expressed feelings of isolation and loneliness.

The fierce independent American spirit and quest for financial security leaves many Americans materially wealthy but spiritually empty and lonely. We live in an extremely busy society where people rush from one commitment to another. Gone are the days of extended families living under one roof and horses and buggies passing in the streets where people could greet one another. Things moved at a much slower pace back then. Nowadays it isn't uncommon for people to go days or even weeks without ever seeing or speaking to their neighbors. Privacy fences and garages allow people to come and go without ever having face-to-face encounters.

In addition, people no longer live in one place all of their lives. Job transfers often require that they move away from friends and family, and though they may pride themselves in their independence, in reality people may feel cut off from the world. America was built on the pioneer spirit, one of independence and self-sufficiency. All of these combined factors make it difficult to feel a sense of belonging. Inwardly they may ask, "Does anyone really care?"

Janet called Wendy, a friend she hadn't spoken with in awhile, and learned that Wendy was experiencing this sense of disconnectedness. At the core of these feelings of isolation was a painful divorce. "How are things going?" Janet asked.

"I just can't seem to feel connected at my church," Wendy said. She explained that rather than go to the church she had been attending while married, she felt it would be less awkward to start afresh. (Her husband still attended the previous church.) At her new church she served in several places—singing in the choir, helping with Vacation Bible School, and attending Sunday School, but she still felt isolated and detached.

Her new church was large. Her Sunday School class had as many as 50 to 75 people on a given Sunday. The large size prevented people from sharing on anything but a surface level. When Janet asked Wendy if her church had small groups, she was surprised to hear that they didn't. Wendy wrestled with what to do and considered church-shopping again. A divorce recovery group or group for older singles might have been a better fit, connecting her with people in similar circumstances.

People need to be needed and accepted. The search for that sense of family and belonging brings many people to church in the first place. If they don't feel they fit in within the first couple of visits, they will often move on. Those who stay, but remain only a part of the crowd rather than integrating into the core, usually experience disconnectedness and discontent. Churches that know how to connect their members instill in them a sense of belonging. These churches do better at retaining individuals for the long term.

Preventing exits from the church community is possible when we involve people in ministry opportunities shortly after their arrival. Even though Wendy felt out of place at her new church, some of her felt needs were being met through serving. This contributed to her loyalty despite her ambivalence. Volunteer opportunities allow people to give something back and to feel needed. When they know others are counting on their service, they become reliable, consistent members. Even more importantly, volunteering facilitates connecting with other people. Yet volunteering alone doesn't always fulfill the connection need.

Small groups can meet this felt need for belonging on a more intimate level. One of Jeff Stewart's roles as pastor of discipleship and small groups at Northgate Christian Fellowship is overseeing small groups and their development. When asked to explain why small groups are so important to the health of a church body, Jeff observes, "Small groups allow for a more concentrated form of ministry to be accomplished. People cannot build up and utilize intimate trust levels in other church venues."

Every church, no matter its size, can benefit from small groups. The larger a church grows, the more crucial it is to have them, because the sense of alienation increases with the size of the church body. Can you think back to an experience of coming to a church for the first time and not knowing anyone? Now imagine coming back the next week and the next. You are only going to get to know people during or after the service, with perhaps only 5 to 10 minutes of socializing, maybe seeing different people each time. A typical worship service experience provides a scant chance for getting to know and bond with the other church attendees. Relationships remain surface.

That sense of disconnectedness leads to becoming a missing-in-action member. Attendance will be spotty at best, and people may drop off the radar screen completely. Their needs are more likely to be met in a small-group setting than in a large group. "The potential for meeting people's needs is much higher in a small-group setting (face to face vs. face to back of head)." So reads a clever quote on New Hope Community Church's small-group Web page, an extension of their church's main Web page. New Hope, based in Walnut Creek, California, realizes that a worship service only affords people the opportunity to get to know the back of the head of the person who sits in front of them. Community is surface level because of insufficient time for relationships to expand to anything else.

Another benefit of small groups is that responsibility for shepherding and caring for the flock is taken off the shoulders of paid staff and placed elsewhere—a very biblical model. When Moses felt overwhelmed by his duties caring for the Israelites, Jethro, his savvy father-in-law, suggested that he assign people to oversee and make judgments over small groups of people (see Exod. 18:13-27). This allowed Moses to tend to other matters.

Church staff must equip members to lead, yet many staff members get sidetracked with managing details that members could actually handle. Churches with small-group leaders free their staff to fulfill other areas of administrative and leadership responsibilities.

So, Uh, What's a Small Group?

Jesus carefully chose specific people to mentor. Plenty of others were in His circle of influence, but these 12 He handpicked. Jesus knew the importance of discipling others so that Kingdom work became easier. He knew that the time He spent coaching these leaders would eventually pay off. With more leaders, more people could be reached and developed into mature Christ followers.

The 12 disciples composed a small group. Jesus cultivated His friendship with them, shepherding them, training them as leaders, and sharing spiritual insights with them. He ate with them. He prayed with them and for them. He did fun things with them, found himself frustrated by them, and helped carry their burdens. He even found support from them (on a good day), and He encouraged and supported them.

Jesus' front-end ministry had back-end results. Most of the men in which Jesus invested His time and energy became leaders, though not all were as well known as Peter, Matthew, Mark, James, and John. The others, except for Judas, faded into obscurity for the most part. Little is written about them, except for Judas who achieved his own level of notoriety, yet imagine how things might have turned out if Jesus had not invested in relationships with the Twelve.

Small groups are exactly what the name says—groups that have a small membership. Although their small size is a common denominator, small groups can be as varied as the flowers in the field. A group's purpose and demographics determine what the group looks like.

Affinity groups are the essence of groups with a unique and specific purpose. John,* an acquaintance of mine, participated in an affinity group. After months of attending a men's Bible study, John still didn't click with the other group members. Eventually he dropped out of the group. Months later he began working with his church's audiovisual team. The group met weekly for planning, troubleshooting, small-group Bible study, and fellowship. He immediately felt at home and became a committed and active member. The group's primary purpose was to create audiovisuals for worship, but they also incorporated Bible study into their meetings. John felt an immediate sense of belonging.

---

*Not his real name.

A couple who had already raised one teen and were in the process of raising two more learned the value of affinity groups as well. Though they were seasoned parents, the ups and downs of dealing with teenage issues and challenges seemed nearly insurmountable. When the parents chatted with other parents of teens at their church, they found that these parents were also struggling in similar areas. They decided that the best solution, since no group like this already existed in their church, was to start a group for parents of teens. Before long, the new group's membership exploded, primarily because so many people wanted to participate in such an affinity group.

Many different types of affinity groups exist, and these special-interest groups are having a powerful impact on those who participate in them. We'll look at these more closely in chapter 5, but suffice it say that if your church doesn't already have some of these special-interest groups, it is well worth considering launching some.

They Come with Benefits

Small groups provide a climate where people can move from surface relationships to something deeper. With these deeper relationships come:

A safe environment for support. Many people believe that depending on others is a sign of weakness. Such independence most likely comes from pioneer days when settlers homesteaded in remote locations relying on their own resources for survival. Survivalist pride lingers today and has raised barriers preventing people from getting to know each other.

Healthy small groups excel at breaking down the walls of self-sufficiency that people erect. People hesitate to reveal what is under the surface until they feel they can trust the person with whom they've been asked to share. As group members come to know each other and grow more comfortable, they begin to open up. Trust builds slowly.

One member may decide to risk sharing something semirisky of a somewhat private nature. Other members watch and see how that information is handled by group members. If they feel comfortable that their issues and secrets will be safe, then they will also begin to let down their guard and reveal their thoughts.

Praying for and supporting each other is one of the most beneficial and beautiful things about small-group ministry. Group members become the family members people often long for but may not have close by. Galatians 6:2 reminds us to "carry each other's burdens."

In my own family, frequent relocations physically separating us from some of our most loved and extended family members have been necessary due to my husband's job. Many times I have felt closer to the members of my small group than I have to my own family members. This is not surprising considering the words of Jesus in Matt. 12:50: "For whoever does the will of my Father in heaven is my brother and sister and mother." Our love for Jesus Christ unites us and makes us one. With a commitment to follow Christ, we become part of a larger family.

Assistance with helping members explore biblical principles. Attending a worship service once a week gives attendees some biblical foundations, but it doesn't allow them to learn on a deeper level. Church members lack the opportunity to turn to the person in the pew and discuss their observations and thoughts on a particular scripture passage. (Well, actually they can, but the pastor might not appreciate it.)

Proverbs 27:17 says, "As iron sharpens iron, so one man sharpens another." In other words, when we are exposed to others and their skills and knowledge, we sharpen our own biblical skills and knowledge and vice versa. A small group is the optimal place for this.

Today's churches face an enormous challenge of educating members about the Bible. Leadership should never assume that the people who attend their services remember the scriptural principles their parents taught them or that they learned in Sunday School. Nor should they assume that people are picking up scriptural knowledge from sermons once a week. If they come that often, they may very well be. Fewer and fewer people, however, have church backgrounds, and many today are biblically illiterate.

Even well-loved Bible stories that seasoned Christians have known since childhood may be totally new stories to many church members. James may not have heard of King David or be familiar with what a synagogue is. Elizabeth may never have heard any of the parables. We are living in the postmodern age. Not only do many people pull their religious viewpoints from a variety of religions and belief systems (many of them non-Christian), but they are often unfamiliar with even basic scriptural references as well. Providing a biblical foundation is more important than ever. Healthy small groups encourage members to use God's Word as their foundation when searching for answers to life's struggles. Groups that teach members to look up scripture passages, question, and probe God's Word are not only equipping members but also laying a foundation vital for solid leadership.

A greenhouse environment for growth and maturity. Gardeners know that a crop of healthy plants comes from cultivating the soil and creating the right environment. To avoid stunted growth, the garden must nurture seeds with rich soil, fertilizer, and water.

Small groups create this same type of nurturing environment for participants. Members need good soil (a healthy small group for starters), fertilizer (getting into God's Word and studying God's Christian principles), and water (instruction and exhortation) to make them grow. A savvy small-group leader creates a hothouse environment for members who look to the leader for godly behavior and principles. Members also benefit from cross-pollination as they discuss spiritual insights and encouragement with other members.

A place for training and equipping leaders and teachers. As a parent I was amazed at how often my immediate family members still expected me to take care of them, exhibiting a "Feed me; I'm helpless" attitude. I jokingly call this the baby bird syndrome. They behaved in this manner well past infancy, even as teens. I knew it wasn't healthy to treat them like baby birds. At some point birds must grow up and take care of their own needs.

To help them mature I've maneuvered them out of the dependency mode, taking deliberate steps to guide them toward maturity and self-sufficiency. Small-group leaders can also benefit from guiding their members toward maturity.

Leaders can't and shouldn't do all the work of the group themselves. Teaching group members to do their share moves them out of the baby bird mode and toward maturity. One of the main reasons churches should have a small-group ministry is to develop mature Christians who will become future leaders.

If you don't want a church full of baby birds, you must work on developing mature Christians. The more members grow toward maturity, the more leaders you cultivate. Small groups are often one of the easiest places to find and develop budding Christian leaders.

Allowing group members to try their hand at teaching and leading can build confidence and skill. We'll look more at leader development in future chapters.

Selling Members and Leaders on Their Value

Launching small groups, particularly in churches that have none or few, can be a daunting task. Just as gardeners first prepare the soil by tilling it and then adding fertilizer, your job will be easier if you first prepare the hearts of leaders and members before starting to build your small-group ministry.

Promote the need. It's easy to think that launching a small-group ministry requires nothing more than starting one small group. Then other people see what a successful group looks like and decide to either join it or start more groups on their own. Occasionally this is the case, but more often than not, a single new group starts without proper support or promotion, then quickly shrivels and dies.

In order for a wide-spread small-group ministry to succeed in a church, people must become active supporters, recognizing within themselves a need for fellowship and spiritual development. It's the task of a church's core leadership to point out this need. Once members are aware of the deficit in their own lives, they recognize that small groups can meet that need.

Sell core leaders on the value. Before you invest much time in small-group development, talk it up to core leaders. Sell the value of small groups with visionary statements or practical illustrations of their importance. Don't expect the message to stick after only one discussion. Several talks may be needed to promote the idea. I've heard that it takes about 10 times to actually convey a new idea. We'd like to think someone understands our idea and that saying it once or twice makes the message clear, but often the picture we reveal is fuzzy.

Your church has influential core leaders. Approach these leaders first. Choose one power monger with whom you have the best rapport, preferably one who has the lead pastor's ear. Invite the leader out for coffee. Explain why small groups can make a difference, their value to your church body, and that the interest in small groups must start with people in the hub.

Ask this leader for suggestions on how to motivate other key leaders to see the importance of small groups. You may need to hold a meeting with these leaders to talk about small groups, or perhaps you might meet with your church board. Talking with the senior pastor may also help. Find someone to partner with who will help move the idea into the hearts and minds of key players.

You may have seen a game called gossip or telephone. Someone starts with a statement and then passes that statement down to each consecutive person. Often, by the time it makes it to the end of the line, participants have lost the original message. To avoid a similar loss in communication, explain the concept clearly to your one key player; then meet with additional leaders to explain it again so that it remains clear and undistorted. Promote small-group participation among your leaders so that the excitement becomes contagious. If you can convey the vision and importance to core leaders, their enthusiasm will be catching to the rest of your members.

Your next step is to preach it and teach it to the church body. Talking about the value of small groups from the pulpit is a simple but effective way. Consider scheduling a sermon series with illustrations and scriptures about the value of small groups. Some scriptures you may want to consider are these: Acts 4:32-35 details how early believers became one in heart and mind and how they cared for one another. Matthew 17:1-13, the story of the Transfiguration, is an example of small groups, because Jesus met with Peter, James, and John in a more intimate setting as a way of mentoring and praying together with them. Note that Jesus purposely separated out three from the other nine: "After six days Jesus took with him Peter, James and John the brother of James, and led them up a high mountain by themselves" (v. 1).

Romans 12:10-16 explains how God designed the Body of Christ to support and encourage each other:

> Be devoted to one another in brotherly love; give preference to one another in honor; not lagging behind in diligence, fervent in spirit, serving the Lord; rejoicing in hope, persevering in tribulation, devoted to prayer, contributing to the needs of the saints, practicing hospitality. Bless those who persecute you; bless and do not curse. Rejoice with those who rejoice, and weep with those who weep. Be of the same mind toward one another (NASB).

By divine design believers are to be not only a spiritual care network that helps us persevere but also a physical care network that covers emotional and practical needs.

In Heb. 10:25 Paul reminds us of the importance of meeting together for support and encouragement: "Let us not give up meeting together, as some are in the habit of doing, but let us encourage one another—and all the more as you see the Day approaching." This verse stresses the value of meeting together and caring for one another and can be coupled with other "one another" verses examined in chapter 15. All are appropriate for use in a sermon or sermon series for educating members about small groups and persuading them to participate in them.

Lydia and several other women were in the habit of gathering together as a group to worship beside the river (Acts 16:13). The church in Philippi started by meeting in homes. Lydia's was one of them (vv. 15, 40). We'll take a more in-depth look at Lydia in chapter 2.

Use several promotional venues to make your campaign more successful. If some small groups are already established, consider inviting one or two members from these groups to speak during the worship service about how small groups have changed their lives. Recorded videos of small-group member interviews and activities impact many. Our church has used these very successfully. Be creative. Consider presenting a drama that highlights the value of small groups. Promote small groups in your newsletter and printed bulletins. Put info about them on the church's Web site (if you have one).

Some churches include in a bulletin insert the names and subjects of their small groups, the day groups meet, and a contact name and phone number. One large church in the Bay area publishes small-group descriptions and contact info on their Web site. Putting crucial info into the hands of members makes connecting them to groups much easier. (Since Web site info is broadcast all over the world, however, you may need to guard privacy by either getting permission from leaders to use their contact info or by opting to list your church phone for contact, thus bypassing any privacy issues.) Make it as easy as possible for members to connect.

Again, you'll be most successful getting people to participate in small groups if you first convince core leaders of their importance. But a creative promotion in the church should directly follow. Even after you start promoting small groups, periodically reminding members about them helps keep people interested in them.

Small groups do not magically salve away all of your church's ailments, but they can promote a more spiritually healthy church body that feels connected, loved, and valued.

Points to Ponder
A Closer Look at Small Groups

1. Think of people you know who belong to different churches. Do their churches have small groups? If so, what are they called (i.e., small groups, core groups, etc.)?

2. How are the small groups of other churches like the small groups at your church (if your church has small groups)? How are they different?

3. If you could take the best qualities of each of these groups and merge them into one group, what would they include?

2 a snapshot of healthy small groups

> The home is still the primary meeting place
> for the church that seeks to unleash believers
> for ministry in one another's lives and
> into the community reaching the
> unsaved for Christ.
> —From the Small Group Page of Oakbrookchurch.net[1]

A large church hosted a small-group fair to help connect people with small groups and to develop new small groups. As a result of the event, several new small groups formed. Sam and Karen* attended this small-group event and connected with a group that met near where they lived. As new Christ followers, they were excited about the opportunity to learn more about God's Word and connect with other believers on a deeper level than during weekend services.

Starting out, their new group was exciting and fun because of all the new friends, but before long, the couple saw serious problems with the group operation. The leader never divided up responsibility. She did it all—hosting the meetings, providing refreshments, and teaching the lesson. The leader was biblically knowledgeable, but her lecture-style format stifled Sam and Karen's need to ask questions about the Scriptures.

The study seemed disorganized and sometimes the leader didn't prepare a lesson, blaming it on her busy schedule. Meetings often ran quite late, a problem for couples like Sam and Karen with younger children who needed to be in bed early. As the months passed, she seemed to put less effort into the lessons, an indicator of leader burnout.

Though Sam and Karen were unhappy with the way the group was being

---

*Not their real names.

managed, they had never participated in a small-group study before and had nothing to compare it to. They persevered for as long as they could before dropping out. Fortunately, they eventually connected with another group that was being managed well. This new group gave Sam and Karen the opportunity to view what a healthy—though not perfect—small group could look like. The group leaders didn't mind if members asked questions about passages they were reading, and they always had a well-planned study. Like a breath of fresh air, it invigorated Sam and Karen.

Vital Signs

Our bodies need nutrients and exercise to be healthy. Small groups within the church body need similar nutrients and care for them to be healthy. An unbalanced and poorly managed group can actually harm the spiritual growth of its members. Just as a physician or nurse might take your pulse, look into your eyes, and check your ears and reflexes to make certain you are healthy, you will want to check your small group's health to see how the group is doing.

Some experts believe that the ideal small group incorporates worship, prayer, community, Bible study, and outreach. Limitations, however, with group meeting times can make it nearly impossible for a group to balance all of these elements. They are still good objectives to try to reach, but groups that cannot achieve all of them should not be discouraged.

Most often worship and outreach are the elements small groups have difficulty incorporating. Meetings simply do not allow time to hit on each one. Nevertheless, you can still work in these elements upon occasion. (We'll cover group health, evangelism, and caring more in depth in another chapter.)

Regarding worship, most small-group members attending weekend worship services are exposed to a specific format. Our idea of worship is often skewed because of what we are accustomed to from earlier experiences. When we mention *worship,* people often think of singing praise songs. Periodically focusing on worship in small groups can teach members that worship also encompasses prayer, selflessness, service, and reverence for God. Worship is an attitude.

Special activities to facilitate worship can be occasionally included in groups. A small group could suspend its regular content periodically and have a musical praise time, or it could devote additional time for prayer and praise. One small group dedicated an evening to reviewing the Lord's Prayer and learning how to pray using the ACTS model of adoration, confession, thanksgiving, and supplication. Small groups that know how to worship are on their way to being deeper, healthier groups.

Warts and All

The personality of the leader impacts the small group. Members need to feel that they can be themselves and that they are free to express their own personalities. This will not happen immediately because members will sense a need to build up the trust level. Authenticity starts with the leader. If a leader is willing to peel back the veneer, then group members may do the same.

A small group chose a new study after completion of their old one. One of the topics was on healing past wounds. The book asked group members to reflect on disappointments and hurts in their lives, and the group hoped to talk about this as well as the book the next time they met.

Their leader anticipated that inducing members to divulge such personal information would be difficult. He planned for this with an icebreaker and asked members to talk about either their most embarrassing moment or something that few people knew about them. He assured members that no one had to talk who wasn't comfortable doing so.

The leader immediately put everyone at ease by relating his own humorous story of an embarrassing moment. Soon others joined in and recounted their own memories. Following this exchange, the group began to talk about deeper revelations. Because members had first exchanged more lighthearted information, they were more willing to open up, taking their cue from the group leader.

Once a leader lets down his or her guard and divulges genuine struggles, others will feel free to eventually pull off their masks and talk about deeper matters. To build healthy relationships, leaders must be authentic and vulnerable. It's risky because someone may not understand. But it is worth the risk to develop genuine trust so that members feel safe sharing deeper concerns.

Group members want someone to look up to and to follow. A leader who constantly wrestles with airing deep issues at small-group meetings may cause group members to question his or her ability to lead. Members may see it as a sign of weakness. Authenticity has its benefits, but too much vulnerability and authenticity has drawbacks. A leader's challenge is to strike a balance, exhibiting strength, authenticity, and vulnerability. By doing so, the group will respect him or her and, in turn, feel free to be authentic as well.

Caring Communities

The early New Testament Church proved itself a caring community. Believers' love and devotion to one another shone out, contagious and inspiring. Everything they had they shared, praying for each other and reaching out to help others. Healthy small groups develop both inward-reaching ways to care for group members and outward-reaching methods to go beyond themselves and show care to others outside. Healthy groups impact both their members and their church.

Inward and Outward Reaching

Most churches have systems in place to care for the spiritual, physical, and even sometimes material deficits of members. This might be achieved through prayer ministry, hospital visitation, and benevolence care that covers material needs upon occasion. But the larger a church grows, the more difficult it is to meet these needs. Small groups can provide for these concerns on a small scale by overseeing the welfare of its members. It may include praying for prayer requests and health issues of members, bringing food to members' families when someone is ill, and even grieving with members who have lost loved ones. Groups are a family in and of themselves.

A small group stepped into a surrogate mother capacity when one of its members had to go away for an extended stay to receive treatment for a serious health issue. Group members brought meals, helped care for the children of the family, and provided transportation for the children and the mother when needed. Members even helped with housecleaning. They stood in the gap as family.

As previously mentioned, healthy small groups also learn how to take that care outside of their tight circle so that through them Christ's love touches the lives of others, even nonchurch members. Healthy small groups know that being a holy huddle is not what God intends, and they strive to stretch beyond comfort zones to reach out to others.

Limited in Size

"Why can't our group be any size we want?" I've heard several group members ask. Your group *can* be any size, but in reality the dynamics change when groups are less than 5 people or larger than 12. Ideally, small groups should be composed of no more than 5 to 12 people.

Professional speaker Brenda Nixon says, "Whether you're leading a Bible study, divorce recovery workshop, or weight-loss class, the ideal size is 12 people. The larger the group, the less individuals open up. It is your responsibility to be aware of this dynamic and attempt to ease a hesitance to contribute."[2]

A group composed of less than 5 people may actually have time for more sharing, but the group's small size means it will have fewer resources from which to draw, including fewer people to contribute to teaching, hosting, and meeting member needs. On the other hand, groups that grow beyond 12 members experience other challenges. Members of larger groups are less likely to communicate beyond the surface level because they are often uncomfortable about taking such a risk in a less intimate environment.

Space may become a problem if you are meeting in homes. Time also becomes an issue because more members mean more people wanting to communicate their needs and concerns. Even managing prayer requests can be tricky with less time to discuss member needs.

Our small group learned some valuable lessons about this when we nearly doubled in size after promoting our group at a ministry fair. We wanted to keep an open membership policy so anyone could join but wrestled with many issues created by the larger group size. Our solution was to divide the group.

We'll talk more later about the pros and cons of open and closed groups (which affect size) and how to multiply groups.

Willing to Share Duties

The leader of the first group that Sam and Karen attended experienced leader burnout. Perhaps this was because she did not know how to delegate responsibility or because she feared what would happen if she relinquished control to someone else. Sharing duties within a small group can be very beneficial.

For one thing, it prevents leaders from exhausting themselves by doing everything. Some of the duties that can be divided up include hosting where the group meets, teaching the lesson, choosing and/or purchasing study materials, and even planning special events. Leaders who familiarize themselves with the unique spiritual gifts and skills of group members can better understand how members are gifted and can determine how to use them. We'll talk more in-depth about spiritual gift assessment in a later chapter.

Leaders who invite group members to help with group duties, making known where and how to help, equip those members to become facilitators. They should not be timid about asking group members to do their share. For instance, they might circulate a signup sheet where members can volunteer to teach a lesson, host the study, or provide refreshments. Doing so teaches both the leader and the members to move past the Lone Ranger mode of operation that declares, "Never mind, I'll do it myself" or "He's the leader, so I don't have to do anything."

Giving group members the opportunity to participate in this way also creates a sense of ownership. If members have responsibilities, they will be more faithful in attending. Group members never asked to do anything often have sporadic attendance. They may treat the group like a convenience store, assuming its services will be available when and if they need to drop in.

Nurturing

Does your church work to develop fully devoted followers of Christ? Do your small-group leaders and members know how to have a good relationship with God? If they do, then they are on the right track. Healthy small groups know the importance of cultivating and developing members to be mature Christ followers. They should provide an atmosphere and climate where people can grow in their depth of knowledge with God. This means choosing study materials that focus and expound on God's Word, stress the importance of spiritual growth and personal development as Christians, and encourage and facilitate prayer life.

Every group takes on a different character influenced by a leader's style and teaching methods. Some groups may choose to study the Bible with no other reference books, and this is fine, if a leader is able to dig down and pull out biblical truths and then make them relevant and understandable to the group's members. Other groups may prefer to read a book, use a workbook, or view a DVD to learn and grow. Resources chosen will depend on the leader as much as the members to determine what method works best. The most important thing is that this spiritual-maturity teaching is taking place. We'll discuss choosing curriculum more in-depth in a later chapter.

Fun-Loving and Innovative

Someone once said, "All work and no play makes Jack a dull boy." The same can be said of small groups. In addition to being a place where members can grow spiritually, groups can also provide a fun social environment. Scheduling periodic fun events can give members a needed break and provide additional time for socializing.

Groups often have one or two individuals who are naturals at planning social events. Give these members opportunities to shine by allowing them to coplan events with you or take solo command of the details. Events can include anything from backyard cookouts to game nights to fancier gatherings such as dinner theaters or shows. Special events such as these can also be a great way to recruit new members and even draw in unchurched people.

Holding two or three social events a year is a good balance. You don't want too many events, otherwise studies and regular sessions will be disrupted. But periodic ones can lend to the fun and help members draw closer together. This book includes a chapter devoted to social events that your group can participate in for relationship-building, fun, and relaxation.

Just as special events can keep groups lively and enjoyable, encouraging groups to be innovative in their approaches can also add new life to groups.

When groups become set in their ways, they may become dull or stagnant. Some members like routine, while others like to try new things. Leaders who are sensitive to both preferences are wise.

If a group always uses the same type of materials for learning, they might want to try something new like a DVD or workbook, since not every person learns in the same way. Trying new subject matter can also be a big plus. Occasionally varying what a group does and how it is done can make meetings more engaging. For instance, I know of a group that intermittently suspends their regular teaching in order to have a tough questions night so that members can ask tough questions about the Bible. Topics include tough life issues or questions members have wrestled with, such as, "Why does God allow suffering?" or "If God loves everyone, then how can hell exist?"

Innovativeness should be welcome as long as it doesn't disrupt the study. Too much innovation can have a counter effect and may exasperate members when no set schedule or method of operation exists. You'll find some creative ideas in the latter part of this book to help bring freshness to your groups.

Groups in Action

Now that we've talked about what healthy small groups look like, let's take a look at small groups in action. Already we have observed that when Jesus met with His disciples to teach and mentor them, He was essentially leading a small group. Many of the works of service and healing He performed were done in the presence of a small group. Paul and Barnabas started churches that began as small groups that met in homes.

In the previous chapter we talked briefly about Lydia. The Sabbath after Paul and Barnabas arrived in Philippi they wanted to worship God. No official place of worship for Jews or Christians existed, so people gathered by the river and that is where Paul and Barnabas found Lydia and her group of women friends (Acts 16:13-15). Lydia had a heart for God, and gathering together to worship and fellowship was important to her. Though she followed God, she didn't personally know Christ. When she heard Paul speak the gospel message, Lydia recognized it as the missing piece. She made a commitment to follow Christ.

Lydia influenced her household to commit themselves to Christ and profess their faith through baptism. She may have already been teaching them what she knew about God before Paul and Barnabas arrived. The group of women that gathered that day probably included members of her household, relatives, and possibly even business acquaintances. She used small-group gatherings to connect and shepherd her friends and family members.

25

Lydia, a successful businesswoman, used her influence to persuade Paul and several of his party to come and stay at her house. This was the beginning of the church of Philippi. Acts 16:40 says, "After Paul and Silas came out of the prison, they went to Lydia's house, where they met with the brothers and encouraged them." *The brothers* refers to other Christian believers and it appears that Lydia had ongoing small-group meetings in her house.

Lydia's group, one of the earliest known models of Christian small groups, was a nurturing environment for mentoring Christ followers and Christian leaders. Participants in this budding church had a powerful impact on people within their sphere of influence. Small groups continue to influence and change lives for the better. Here are just a few real-life examples of small groups in action.

Giving others a hand up. A women's small group has an outreach ministry for abused women. They collect food and personal hygiene items to deliver to a women's shelter. Not long after starting this ministry, one of the women in the group learned that a local dry cleaner had many nice suits that were unclaimed. A group member arranged to pick up these suits and deliver them to the shelter to be used by women when they went on job interviews.

Being a light to the community. Another small group participated in a community chili cook-off. The proceeds of the cook-off went to support affordable housing. Their participation gave them the opportunity to rub shoulders with other nonchurch members and organizations in the community and be salt and light in their town. In the process, the group made friends with an influential community activist who had been resistant to the church's building program that sought to secure an extension in the urban growth boundary. The existing boundary at the time did not allow for building of any kind.

Though it was not their initial intent, the positive impression group members made on the woman who headed up the cook-off caused her to rethink her position against the building. She later influenced the city counsel to vote in favor of extending the growth boundary for the building program.

Comforting those who grieve. A pastor presiding over his church's annual banquet talked about the year in retrospect, mentioning several church members who had died. A widow of one of the deceased began to quietly weep. Another widow reached over and held her hand. This comforting relationship started through a small group for those who had lost spouses. The group was a place of healing, caring, and support for those who had lost loved ones. The love poured out at the banquet was an outward example of how those needs were being met.

After a young mother miscarried, she had difficulty finding the words to pray. Members of her small group interceded for her and prayed with her. People also responded by providing meals and sending flowers and cards.

Family to those who have none. When the member of a small group who had no family nearby moved from an apartment into her condo, members from her small group provided muscles, trucks, and food on moving day to help her make the transition.

Supporting and encouraging recovery. A participant in a recovery small group sensed a need for a support group for teens of parents who had been substance abusers. He formed a small group especially for teen support.

A woman who struggled with bulimia as a young adult launched a small group for people with eating disorders. The group is just one of many recovery groups based on the 12-step recovery program adapted by Saddleback church for their Celebrate Recovery program. Celebrate Recovery's material is adapted from the Alcoholics Anonymous 12-step program. The same church that hosts the eating disorder group also hosts groups for divorce recovery and substance abuse recovery.

All groups incorporate similar foundational principles based on steps that help individuals recover from abusive or destructive behaviors. The strength of these groups lies in the openness and willingness of group members to admit to specific areas where they struggle to gain control and balance over addictive and self-destructive behaviors. Recovery groups are one the fastest-growing groups in churches today.

Building bridges to connect with nonbelievers. One particular small group was soon drawing non-Christ followers into its group, providing the opportunity to reach beyond church walls with the gospel message.

A retired nurse practitioner wanted to reach out to some women she knew but felt most would probably not come to church if asked. She invited them to her home for dessert and tea, and they watched a motivational tape by a well-known Christian speaker.

Strengthening marriages. When a couple came to a pastor for marital counseling, they asked if a support group for married couples existed. The pastor and his staff had been aware for some time that the church desperately needed such a group. Perhaps this was the time. After talking with staff members and praying over the matter, they publicized the need for a couple to facilitate the group. One couple volunteered to help. Together with the pastors, they researched resources that could be used in leading the group. Before long, a small group formed. The one couple who had originally sought help was able to strengthen their relationship and they are still going strong. Many other couples have benefited as well.

Teaching morality. A couples' small group that included families with teen boys and teen girls dedicated one month to purity. Fathers in the group gathered with their sons for a barbecue, then watched a video on sexual purity.

Women in the group devoted similar bonding time for connecting with their daughters with a comparable lesson. During the remainder of the month, groups continued meetings, devoting the time to help their young adults gain a positive and godly perspective on sex, marriage, and male/female relationships.

We've looked at crucial components that make up healthy small groups and examples of small groups in action. When people come together in the intimate setting of small groups, they develop a sense of community, learning Christ's teachings and imitating those teachings. Though groups may be small numerically, they can still have a profound effect on those they touch. Together, small-group members can change the world, one life at a time.

Points to Ponder
Checking Your Groups' Health

1. Do you belong to a small group? If so, review the attributes of healthy small groups that we discussed in this chapter. List the areas below where you feel the group you belong to is most healthy:

   List the areas where you feel your group needs to improve:

2. Look at the small groups your church hosts as a whole.

   List the areas below where you feel your group is most healthy:

   List the areas where you feel your group needs to improve:

3. Name three people you know of who have benefited from small groups.

   How have the groups helped them?

3 laying the groundwork

What is the purpose of your group?
Whatever you choose, make it clear.
—Dan Chun[1]

At a small-group leader networking session, leaders talked about some of the biggest triumphs and challenges they experienced while facilitating small groups. Leaders had many positive things to say, and they shared similar concerns pertaining to small groups.

Common issues included coping with small-group members who monopolized discussion time, getting members involved in leadership, determining how to provide child care for members, motivating quieter members to participate in discussion, and keeping attendance steady.

Several seasoned leaders gave similar counsel. They advised that many of the problems newer groups and novice leaders faced could be curbed by developing mission statements, group guidelines, and core values. Experience had taught them that written rules and regulations decreased most troublesome issues because both group members and facilitators knew what to expect.

Teams and boards without clear boundaries and goals typically struggle toward a common purpose. Productivity suffers. Small groups with no mission statement or guidelines struggle in a similar way because they lack clarity of purpose.

Though small groups, teams, and boards differ substantially, they share some similar dynamics. All involve a variety of personalities with numerous expectations and needs. When gathered together, the differences can quickly lead to friction and then frustration. Members may either try to control group meetings and turn them in the direction they think they should go or opt out of future participation.

Groups need not have written guidelines. Many small groups operate without them, but guidelines help decrease chaos and conflict. Guidelines help answer the who, what, where, when, how, and why of a group. By addressing these questions ahead of time, you decrease confusion about the group's purpose and function.

Beginning with a Mission

Group guidelines act as a road map to help a group stay on track. Before your small group sets out on its journey, you'll need to get a compass reading. A mission statement points your group in the right direction, acting as the *what* of a group, defining its purpose and focus.

A few years ago I helped found our church's Ministry Team. Starting out, I believed my goals were clear; however, I found that writing them down forced me to condense and clarify. I knew that our church could benefit from a team that networked ministry openings with volunteers and facilitated ministry. I, and several other leaders, defined the team purpose.

"What exactly is it we are trying to accomplish?" we asked. We had to convey that purpose and mission to other team members we hoped to recruit, so it needed to be clear and easy to grasp. We wanted to make certain we were all working toward the same goal.

My team members agreed that the team aimed to promote and facilitate ministry. But that definition remained vague. As we worked through the team's identity on paper and dry erase board, we discovered we had four purposes. The first excited people about serving, the second taught them how to pinpoint their gifts and abilities, the third assisted with connecting them to ministry opportunities that matched their interests and gifts, and the fourth promoted ministry opportunities so that more people got involved.

Experience has taught me that having a clearly written mission statement empowers team members to focus in on what the team is trying to accomplish. Without guidelines, meetings run on indefinitely, and people chase rabbits all over the field. Those who give up their time to attend come away frustrated when their expectations are not realized or no sense of accomplishment rewards them. They may want to contribute, but a lack of focus prevents them. The secular workforce recognizes the importance of having a written agenda at team meetings. It does wonders for keeping meetings on track.

The book writing process provides another example. When a writer conceives an idea for a book, he or she has to pitch the idea to an editor to capture the editor's interest. Seasoned writers know that a short, one-paragraph synopsis about their book's thesis is the beginning of an excellent book proposal. If a writer can't clearly focus the book idea, chances are the proposal and book manuscript won't be focused either. That one paragraph synopsis is very similar to a mission statement.

Just as a mission statement helps teams and boards pin down and stick to their purpose and function, a clearly focused synopsis helps writers zero in on their book's purpose. A small-group mission statement tells its members why the group exists. That clearly focused and condensed one- to two-sentence statement makes it easy for group members and leaders to explain the purpose to new group prospects by using the mission statement. Potential new members can determine whether this particular group fits their interests and needs and lines up with their expectations.

Having a mission statement in place before your first small-group meeting helps to define and shape a group from the start. Members most likely to benefit from and grow comfortable with the group are the ones who opt to attend. You can hammer out group guidelines and core values (which we will talk about soon) after the group starts meeting.

When devising a mission statement, whether for a board, a team, your personal life purpose, or a small group, the highest impact comes if it follows the "three s" rule.

Short. Many churches have mission statements to help leaders and members comprehend the church's specific purpose. I have seen some church mission statements of astounding length. Multiple well-written paragraphs may seem eloquent but may lose the readers in the passages.

Most people have difficulty remembering more than a few sentences. The longer the mission statement, the harder it is to understand and keep in mind. Work to trim your mission statement down to one to two sentences. Why work to make a mission statement memorable? Because people can recall it and repeat it to others.

A lengthy mission statement may indicate a scope that's too broad. Scale down your group's area of focus and limit it to a select few. Make your statement so concise you could explain it to someone in an elevator while gliding to the desired floor.

Simple. Avoid fancy talk, big words, and complicated jargon. Choose words everyone can understand. If they understand, they will remember. As an editor once said, "Never use a dollar word when a fifty-cent word will do. Otherwise you'll lose the audience in the language."[2]

Say it again. It should be repeatable. Some clever people come up with mission statements that are acronyms (a word formed from the first letter or letters of each successive part). For instance, you may have heard of the term KISS. KISS is an acronym often used by people in the business world to remind them to Keep It Simple Stupid. I'm not suggesting that you make this your mission statement, but it gives you a sample of an acronym.

For instance, a group concerned with showing care and compassion to others might choose the initials TLC, a common abbreviation for tender loving care. They might change it to say their mission is Teaching, Love, and Community.

Mission statements can also use alliteration, which is repeating the first consonant sounds in two or more words (or syllables) that are close to each other. Because of the repetition of sounds, people remember this group's name: Sharing, Repairing (bringing healing to members), and Caring (reaching out in missions). Alliteration techniques make the mission statement easy to remember and repeat.

If a person can easily remember a small group's mission statement, the members can easily understand their group's purpose and convey their purpose to both members and prospective members.

Sample Mission Statements

Below are some actual small-group mission statements. Small groups from different churches used these flyers to promote their groups. The group names appear first, followed by their mission statement.

Metamorphosis. Metamorphosis has a twofold purpose: (1) **Maturity:** to grow and mentor Christ followers to become mature Christians, using God's Word as adviser and compass. (2) **Ministry:** to develop, equip, and encourage the leader in every believer so that he or she can bring others into a mature relationship with Christ.

Northgate Support Group. Our purpose is to serve the single-parent community so that they might:

• Engage in a personal relationship with God
• Nurture their children in love and discipline
• Encourage one another to grow spiritually, emotionally, and socially

Wednesday Night Small Group. We review the pastor's sermon message outline and discuss how it applies to our daily lives.

Christian Educators in Prayer. Our purpose is to:

• Pray for students.
• Pray for parents.
• Pray for schools.
• Pray for our communities.

Single Purpose. We apply God's Word to daily situations facing single adults. We also host events and activities in order to provide fellowship and joy with each other living in the light of God's presence (see 1 John 1:5-7).

Seasons. A group for adults over 50 who wish to study and fellowship together. Our purpose is to grow old gracefully while growing in maturity spiritually.

Impact. Our purpose is to grow spiritually through the study of God's Word so that we develop into mature Christians who impact others.

Mentors. Equipping fathers to raise whole-hearted followers of Christ.

These are fine examples of effective mission statements. Again, the key is to be as precise and brief as possible.

The Name Game

Some groups consider their name central to their existence, while others appear unconcerned with what they call themselves. Sometimes small groups adopt the name of the night or day on which they meet or the subject the group studies, such as Wednesday Night Men's Group or the Saturday Morning Women's Group.

The right group name made a world of difference to a small group I facilitated. When the group started, we called ourselves Leaders on Purpose, and our mission/purpose was basically the same as the Metamorphosis group's (shown on the previous page). We wanted our group to train and nurture leaders to Christian maturity and to challenge people to take on leadership roles. The group stayed open to anyone, but the name Leaders on Purpose deterred people who believed they had to already be in a leadership role or have strong leader qualities to join.

Soon 12 regular members came. Many were core church leaders, but not all. Everyone was, however, already highly involved in serving the church in some way.

Before our church held a ministry fair, I asked members if they thought we should change our name. The primary reason was because people still had a misconception of the group's purpose. Group members discussed our name and whether to change it. Members favored choosing a new name that would appeal more to the general public. We batted around several ideas, settling on Metamorphosis. The group's general mission and makeup remained the same, but Metamorphosis reflected our desire to grow and change into mature Christians as a butterfly transforms from a chrysalis.

At the small-group promotional event we had a butterfly on our flyer as a symbol of Christian transformation. Not long after the event, we doubled in size. I suspect the increase in size was due to our name change. People found it appealing (or maybe they just liked butterflies).

Names can and will make a difference. A group name should not only describe the group but also have appeal and reflect the group's mission/purpose. So it's best to craft a group's mission statement first and arrive at the name afterward. If a leader settles on a name and finds later it misleads potential members into thinking the group is something it is not, it might be appropriate to change it.

Some groups name their group after a particular study. A group studying biblical precepts (principles) might call itself Precepts. A group studying Exodus calls itself Exodus. When these groups complete their studies, their names will no longer fit. If they change their names, people may become confused because they think it is a different group because the name is unfamiliar.

Choosing a group name is similar to choosing a business name. If the name is too specific, it locks a group into a really tight focus. If it's broad, people won't have a clear idea of what the group offers. Try to choose a name specific enough that it ties into the group's mission but general enough that it can change and grow with the group, its mission, and its purpose.

Here are just a few group names that small groups have chosen to use:

F-I-S-H (Friends Intimately Seeking Him)

Exalt

Spread the Word Network

Aspire

Phileo Phish

Road Trip

Prime Time (ages 40 and above)

Rooted in the Spirit

Overflow

Living Stones

Glue

Eleventh Hour Recovery

Footprints

Super Girls

Young Professionals

J. C.'s Crew (for teens)

Helmsmen (for men)

Young at Heart (retirees)

The Hot Tea Ladies

Setting Guidelines and Core Values

Establish group guidelines, or rules of operation, the first time a small group meets. If the leader has done his or her homework, the group will already have a mission statement. At the group's first session, the leader can start with introductions of members and then read the mission statement, explaining that the group needs to work together to come up with guidelines. Members may question why guidelines are necessary, especially free-spirit types and those who register strongly on the mercy and compassion scale.

Group leaders can explain that these guidelines are for everyone's benefit. By setting boundaries members feel are important, they have a say in how their group operates. For instance, one small group composed of couples with small children agreed that their conclusion time should be at 8:30 P.M., which allowed members enough time to get their younger children in bed for school.

Another group leader suggested that their group establish a rule that required group members to call the leader if they couldn't attend a meeting. In the past, the leader had experienced some frustration after preparing a lesson and getting his home ready for guests, only to have no one show up. Establishing this rule made explicit the courtesy of consideration for those in leadership and hosting positions.

Here are a couple examples from real life where setting new guidelines was called for:

We live in an age of cellular convenience and people are likely to have phone calls at any location at any time. Occasionally a cell phone will go off during our church's worship services (despite reminders to turn them off). Usually after an incident one of our pastors jokingly reminds people that if their cell phone interrupts the service they have to buy pizza for everyone present. (We don't enforce it, but it always gets a laugh and people are more aware of phone etiquette afterward.)

A small group that experienced multiple phone interruptions during their small-group meetings established a rule that no one was allowed to answer the phone during group meetings. Establishing such a rule can help prevent annoying interruptions. Some parents, however, are not comfortable with this because they need to give a babysitter an emergency number. In such cases the leader and members should discuss what rules pertain to phone usage so that all understand the boundaries.

Another example of chaos caused by a lack of boundary guidelines is an incident that occurred in a small group when a mother of young children could not secure her regular sitter the night of her group's meeting. She contacted the group hostess who gave the mother permission to bring her children to the Bible study where the hostess's teen daughter would watch the kids in an upstairs bedroom. The study quickly deteriorated when several of the children ran to their mother in the midst of the study to ask about minor matters. The commotion escalated when the babysitter brought them to the kitchen for a snack. With the kitchen opening into the meeting room, most group members could neither hear nor focus on what the leader was teaching. The four young children drew all of the attention. After the incident the group established a new rule—no child care at the same location of gatherings.

Asking members to suggest values and boundaries for a group's operation can shape mission statements, guidelines, and core values. You'll find a set of questions at the end of this chapter to assist leaders in this process. The questions will help define the how and where (group guidelines) and the what and why (core values). Keep in mind that unlike the mission statement, which defines the group's purpose, the guidelines and core values define what is important to the group.

The promotional flyer of the Metamorphosis group defines the group's core values. Listing these helped prospective members decide if they matched up with the group's interests and focus. Here are some of the core values the group listed.

Core Values of the Metamorphosis Group

- **We love stretching and growing,** so we share teaching and hosting responsibilities and we sometimes take on projects so we can reach out to others in ministry.
- **We love fun,** so we have frequent fun types of events and gatherings.
- **We love food,** so eating and fellowship are a big part of this group.
- **We value learning biblical principles** to apply to our daily lives.
- **We love supporting each other,** so we share prayer requests and concerns because we see each other as family.

Listing a group's core values can help group members understand how the group will operate and what is important to its members while tipping off potential new members about group member values.

The Single Purpose group, previously referenced, is a small group for singles. Their values include having fun social events. They listed these as meals at local restaurants, barbecues, potlucks, hiking, skiing, golf, volleyball, movie nights, sports event outings, dancing, and dance lessons.

The LOFT small group values finding identity in honest, accountable relationships and a place of service. They also reference social activities and monthly fellowship as crucial core elements to their group purpose and identity.

Some groups take their guidelines very seriously and require members to sign an agreement. Then they give each group member a copy. A sample group covenant or agreement that one group used is included at the end of this chapter. Group leaders will be responsible for determining how structured and formal group guidelines should be.

Signing a group agreement impresses on group members the guidelines they helped create so that their group operates more efficiently. Signed agreements also give members a written reminder to keep. Sometimes the formal approach cements this into their memories. Even when members don't sign a contract, reviewing the guidelines with your group and giving members a copy gives them a reminder of how things should operate.

Leaders should periodically revisit their guidelines and mission statement with members for several reasons. First, people have short memories. They may not remember previously agreed upon guidelines. A group that agreed to conclude at 8:30 P.M. so that parents can get their kids to bed on a school night might overshoot the deadlines and adjourn later each week. (People love to talk, and it's easy for the time to pass quickly.) Though it may not bother some members, it becomes an inconvenience and source of irritation for others, especially hosts/hostesses who need to get up early the next day.

Reviewing the guidelines is also wise because group needs are always changing. As new group members join, leaders can provide them with guidelines and restate the group purpose so that they understand the group's mode of operation. (Reviewing also refreshes group members' memories.)

Staying Connected

Group members draw closer as small groups become comfortable with their identity, supporting and fellowshipping with each other. In order to help members stay connected, leaders might consider creating a directory that can be distributed to each member. The directory can include group members' names, addresses, phone numbers, and e-mails. Including the names of children of these families helps also. A directory will help members get to know each other better. E-mails frequently change and people sometimes move, so leaders should periodically update the roster so that new members are listed and changes in contact information are reflected.

Another great aid is an e-mail list. Leaders can periodically send reminders to members about group meeting locations, what lesson the group is on, and what special events are coming up. They can also let the group know about any prayer requests and group needs that have arisen. Groups that meet less than once a week will find this especially helpful, since people often forget when meeting dates are and what locations are scheduled.

Establishing guidelines is strictly optional, but they can make operations run more smoothly. Mapping out group core values and how the group will operate right from the start curbs trouble and frees leaders up to concentrate on teaching, pastoring, and facilitating, rather than on minutiae that can divert a group from its main focus.

A Sample Covenant

Below is a sample covenant we used in our teen parenting group. You can easily adapt and change it to suit your group's needs.

"Stayin' Alive" (Teen Parenting) Small Group Covenant
Creekside Church, Aurora, Colorado
Leaders Jeff and Teena Stewart

1. This group will meet every second and fourth Saturday of each month.
2. We will commence fellowship at 7 P.M.
3. We will alternate hosting by mutual agreement and will notify the participants.
4. This group is open through April 2001 and to parents of teens only. We will not bring our teens/children.
5. We will utilize Christian resources that will lead us to probe God's Word for principles and standards on how to relate with our teenager(s).
6. We will openly share with honesty but maintain confidence with each other.
7. We will try to do something in the way of outreach/mission two times per year.
8. We will schedule social gatherings once per quarter.
9. When we meet, we will most likely have something to eat.
10. We will endeavor to multiply our group by creating apprentice leaders and a new small group.

Signed:

_____

_____

_____

_____

_____

_____

_____

_____

_____

_____

Points to Ponder
Questions for Establishing the Group Mission Statement, Core Values, and Guidelines

Use the questions below to help define a group mission statement, core values, and guidelines.

1. What is this group's purpose?

2. What will the group's name be? Try to tie the group name in with its mission statement/purpose.

3. Where will the group meet?

4. How often will the group meet?

5. On what day of the week will it meet?

6. What time of day will it meet?

7. Will it meet, weekly, biweekly, monthly?

8. Will you have refreshments? If so, who will provide them?

9. Who will lead discussion?

10. What will the group study?

11. Will child care be provided? If so, at what location and how will the sitter be paid?

12. Will this be an open group (always open to new members) or a closed group (limited to x number of members)?

13. What will be the group's starting and ending time?

14. Will the group have social activities? If so, how often?

15. Will the group participate in outreach, benevolence, missions, or evangelism events? If so, how often?

16. What ages can participate in this group (teens, young adult, middle age, older adults, and/or retired adults)?

17. Is the group open to couples, singles, divorcés, and so forth?

18. Is the group open to nonchurch members?

19. Will members need to call if they cannot attend?

20. Will the group work on training apprentice leaders?

4   launching new groups

Each year we have an increase of students and have built
a few groups that meet regularly. That is what is great
about small groups; they are meant to be small!
If there are just a handful in your group who
have some interest, get your stake in
the ground and start with them.
—Todd Szymczak[1]

Years ago, when Jeff and I were new to ministry, we shepherded a small church
in Pennsylvania. When we arrived at the church, only two small groups existed. Retired individuals attended one and older women participated in a
women's Bible study. As our church grew, the numbers of younger couples did
too. Even so, nothing existed for connecting them outside of Sunday worship.
Hoping to meet this need, I decided to launch a couples Bible study. We led
the study, which met in our home.

The group started out fairly strong with about four couples, but the busy
schedules of participants with children competed with the meeting times. Attendance became sporadic. Because of the group's small size, when one couple
missed, everyone felt the absence. Sometimes we were the only ones who
showed up.

After about six months of struggling to hold our group together, we decided to call it quits. People weren't ready. Looking back, with much more experience, I can see many things we did wrong. When trying to launch our group
we overlooked a key principle—the importance of selling our congregational
members on the value of small groups. The hearts of our members were not
ready for small groups because we had not properly prepared them. We failed
to teach them about small-group benefits. The few couples we managed to interest in coming had not fully bought into the benefits. When people don't
catch the vision, the vision usually isn't catching.

Our church never managed to get any more Bible study groups going, and

I believe the gap caused by not having a venue where people could learn and network on a more intimate level contributed to the church's decline. The church closed its doors several years after we left. How is your church doing in relation to small groups? Do your members see groups as an important part of your church's heartbeat? If no groups or only a few exist or those that do are struggling, you have some work to do. Don't despair. You can take steps to prepare the soil.

Getting people to recognize the value and need for small groups starts in the pulpit and classroom. You can motivate members to think about small-group involvement by preaching to them and teaching them about the benefits and values of such groups.

Whenever you want people to embrace a new idea, frequent reminders are often necessary. Promote it from numerous angles. Talk about it with your adult ministry leaders, youth ministry leaders, and children's ministry leaders. Discuss it with your paid and volunteer staff. Create a buzz. Once you get groups up and running, periodically endorse the value of small groups to your congregation so people continue to see their worth.

Leaders and class teachers can also teach about the importance of small groups. Mention small groups and the opportunities they provide in passing when discussing other topics. For instance, if your church has an inquirers' class where people come to learn about your church and its beliefs, work in telling them about small groups and their benefits.

If you have spiritual gifts discovery classes, mention small groups as a way to get connected. Since people are already thinking about getting involved and serving, it can provide more opportunities for them to connect with other church members. Give leaders who teach adult Sunday School classes information on small groups so that class participants know about them. For instance, a leader might hand out flyers to class attendees.

Never assume your congregation knows about small groups and how to get connected. Provide them with ample information. Sell your church leaders on the importance of small groups. Start with core leaders, including staff. Get them to buy into the idea.

And if you are one of the key church leaders and staff members, encourage your colleagues in leadership to participate in small groups. If they do, it will be much easier to get members involved. People are quick to pick up on what they consider to be hypocrisy. If you are touting small groups but your leadership isn't participating in them, don't expect your members to jump on board.

If your church is large enough to have multiple staff members, and you don't already have a small group for them, consider advocating that they start one for staff. A small group for this purpose will give staff firsthand experience and a badly needed support network. (Who better understands the needs of staff than other staff?) Then they, in turn, will be open to the idea of promoting small groups.

Small-group fellowship for staff members and leaders doesn't have to be within your church. Key leaders, especially staff members, aren't always comfortable in small groups with members from their own churches. Members may view and treat them differently—as the hired help or as someone on a pedestal. Staff members may find it difficult to talk about their life struggles and are often careful about what they share.

If small groups from other churches will allow staff members and leaders to participate more openly, then this is an additional consideration for their choice of small-group involvement. The same is true for nonpaid core leaders. Groups for core leaders can provide a nurturing environment for growth and maturity. Once staff members and key leaders participate in small groups, these leaders can motivate other church members to join small groups since they understand and appreciate the benefits firsthand.

When large companies want to promote a product, they hire someone to launch an ad campaign. Well-designed ad campaigns don't involve a single billboard; they utilize a variety of mediums like radio, print, billboards, and other options. The synergy of multiple components working together virtually guarantees successful results.

Your small-group advertising campaign needs to follow the same principle. Use a combination of mediums for promoting small groups. You can do this through sermons, announcements, videos, dramas, flyers, and more. Having someone who is already involved in a successful small group share about how small groups have positively impacted his or her life can generate much interest. Of course, nothing can beat the personal one-on-one invitation.

Experienced ad agents know that it's not the product that sells, but the benefits. If you can sell members on the benefits of small groups and how much they need them, then getting them involved will be easy. Design your campaigns to show the difference small groups can make in people's lives. Brainstorm a number of creative ways to get this point across, then sell, sell, sell so people get excited about joining or starting small groups.

Starting with What You Have

Church size should have nothing to do with the success of your small groups. Some small churches have multiple small groups, while some large churches have only a handful. Small groups, however, are a good indicator of the health of your church.

Don't despair if your church has a minimal amount of groups. Work with what you have. Even one group can be used to start other groups when you take the divide-and-conquer approach. Begin by training your leaders to look for potential small-group leader apprentices.

"Sometimes opportunity is like staring at the knees of a giraffe," observes author/speaker Laurie Beth Jones in her book *Jesus CEO*.[2] We often fail to spot leaders among us because we are standing too close to them and overlook the obvious. We must first *believe* that leaders are present. Once we accept the reality that they exist, our next step is to begin *identifying* them. Noting potential leaders within existing groups helps increase the chances of spawning new small groups by cultivating that leadership potential.

Scouting Out Small-Group Facilitators

Leadership looks different on different people. Some people are outspoken, obvious leaders who command attention. Others are quiet types, working more behind-the-scenes. Start by observing group members. Look for potential apprentices who, with a little coaching, might be able to facilitate a small group in the future. Not every group will have a potential leader apprentice, but most will, and some groups may have several potential leaders.

If you are unsure of what to look for in a potential leader, here are some qualities to consider:

- Dependability—someone who can be counted on
- Maturity—someone who is responsible and growing in his or her relationship with Christ
- Knowledge—someone with a good grasp on Scripture
- Teaching gifts—someone who can convey spiritual principles clearly
- Administration—someone who can organize and manage
- Likeability—someone people enjoy being around
- Leadership—someone people naturally follow
- Credibility—someone whose judgment people trust and follow
- Compatibility—someone who gets along with others and your church's belief system

Traits such as likeability are not enough of a quality to suggest leadership. Many likeable people are not leader material. Likeability, however, is a significant trait to look for in a leader apprentice because group members must respect the leader.

One of the best ways to identify a potential leader is to ask existing leaders (or even group members) to suggest names of people in their groups that exhibit leadership potential. People are often unaware of leader qualities in others until you ask them to reflect on them. Once they begin to observe, it is amazing what they see. Many of the aforementioned traits may be present in some of their small-group members. People with these traits may come to mind because they proved themselves at some point and stand out from other group members in some way.

Leadership traits are crucial to selecting leader apprentices. You should also consider compatibility. Christians come from a variety of church backgrounds, some even from nonchurch backgrounds. In extreme cases, some may come from religions or belief systems better classified as cults. A leader's background may be very different from your church's culture and fundamental beliefs. Don't hold this against them. (Consider the apostle Paul and his transformation.)

Learn as much as you can about a prospective leader's beliefs and background before placing him or her as a group leader. Make sure the person you choose adheres to the nonnegotiables, such as those outlined in the Apostles' Creed. Filter out prospects who seem bent on forcing their own church cultures (narrow, rigid, liturgical, charismatic, etc.) on group members.

At the end of this chapter is a work sheet to help identify potential small-group leaders. Use this tool to reflect on people you might want to groom for leadership positions.

Training Apprentices

Once you've identified potential leaders, your next step is to train them as leader apprentices. A subtle approach often works best. Don't scare off potential apprentices by calling them apprentices to their faces. You don't even have to let them know they are being considered. Quietly identify who might be your leaders and start grooming them to take on more responsibility. Some suggestions for apprentice training include:

- Ask a potential leader to colead or take a portion of the lesson.
- Ask an apprentice leader to lead a lesson. (You might deliberately schedule another commitment for yourself so that you won't be present.)
- Ask the apprentice for input on how the group is being managed.
- Plant the idea in the apprentice's head that he or she might consider leading a group in the future.
- Be available to coach, encourage, and offer pointers when you do give additional responsibility.
- Ask the apprentice if he or she could do anything ministry related, what that would be. (If he or she indicates interest in leading a small group, you've got a ready-made leader!)
- Evaluate how the apprentice does at teaching when given the opportunity. (You may find that some people are not cut out for leadership while others excel at it.)

Once you have identified and begun working with your apprentice, set a goal for when you would like to talk with your apprentice about launching his or her own small group. Offer your mentoring and coaching services to this individual to downplay any fears he or she has of flying solo. Sometimes all a potential leader needs is a little reassurance and experience.

Developing new leaders is one way of setting the stage to launch new small groups. As a small-group champion, you should always be looking for new ways to develop more groups. An easy way of starting small groups is to create spin-off groups. In addition, participating in other more event-oriented activities can assist you with getting new small groups up and running.

Spinning Off Groups

Have you ever been a fan of a popular TV show that ends up birthing a new show? Spin-offs happen when a particular character or star has enough of a popular following that producers are willing to try similar shows based on those characters. *Cheers* gave birth to *Frazier*. *Friends* birthed *Joey*. *Green Acres* birthed *Petticoat Junction*. Just as successful shows spin off other successful shows, you can do the same with small groups, particularly when they grow too large.

I mentioned earlier that the ideal small-group size is no larger than 12. When small groups surpass that number of people, group intimacy becomes difficult. Remember the discussion about the importance of group names? The Leaders on Purpose group experienced a sudden surge in membership after making a name change. Just prior to the name change the group consisted of around 10 members. When the group adopted the new name, several simultaneous events caused the group to swell rapidly.

First, the name change made it more appealing to other potential members. The new name, Metamorphosis, made people feel welcome as individuals (not just leaders). At about the same time the name changed, the group participated in a small-group promotional fair. Every group had flyers displayed on tables, and through this event the group picked up a few more members.

A few weeks after the fair, the church installed a table in the church foyer to promote several of the church's ministries. The table highlighted a different ministry each month. During the month emphasizing small groups, Metamorphosis displayed its flyers alongside those of other small groups. Something about the group focus, the alternating Thursday night format, the new name, and the flyer design appealed to people, and the group gained 9 more members.

Members enjoyed being part of the thriving and growing group, but they felt the strain of the rapid expansion. The group rotated homes, and participants tried to cram into different houses at each meeting. Sometimes they fit well. At other times they were cramped for space, depending on house size and the number of people who came. There wasn't time for everyone to share their comments and prayer requests. Planning special events created more space issues because everyone wanted to attend them.

Shepherding members took an increasing amount of energy even though group members weren't particularly needy, because more people needed attention. A member jokingly referred to the group as their second church, and it was well on the way in size to becoming one.

The member who labeled our group a church was close to the truth. Often, when leaders plant a new church, they start with a core of people from a parent church. Spinning off a small group can be handled in much the same way as planting a church from an existing church body. If you have a large "small group" on the verge of needing to split, present the opportunity to existing members to help plant a new group (once you have chosen a leader). The seed group will be your new group plant.

You'll increase the success of this new spin-off group by continuing to coach the leader. Here are some tips for making your spin-off successful:

- Assure the new group leader that the existing leader will be available to answer questions.
- Give the new group leader a copy of the parent group's guidelines, mission statement, and core values; then offer to be present at their initial meeting to form their own guidelines and core values.
- Offer to help the leader choose new curriculum.
- Provide special event opportunities that the new group and parent group can participate in together so members don't suffer from separation anxiety.
- Encourage the two groups to cross-promote their activities so they share in each others' lives.
- Provide your leader with a hard copy and electronic version of the roster of the parent group's members and contact information. Encourage the leader to create a new roster from the original consisting of members who are to participate in the spin-off group. As new group members join the new group, the leader can add their names to the roster.
- Work with the leader and spin-off group members to choose a name for their group to help form ownership and pride in identity.

Spinning off a group is one of the most natural ways to multiply small groups, but what if groups aren't ready to split? Below are some additional suggestions for helping create and promote small groups.

Small-Group Connections[3]

When Renee Schoenborn moved to the Bay area, someone from her church invited her to attend a small group. "It was the best thing that happened to me," says Renee. "I met 'family.' I didn't have any family in the area. In a small group there's intimacy and someone I can count on and lean on. It wasn't so much the Bible study . . . more the support and relationships and praying for each other."

Lani Sinclair had a similar experience. She missed her extended family in Oklahoma and the church she previously attended. "When I moved here, I plugged into the women's Bible study immediately and loved it. It was just like Renee described it."

Reflecting back, Renee observes, "I felt more at home in Northern California in a year than I did in 10 years in Texas." The church Renee had left behind didn't have small groups. When she visited a small group at her new church, she immediately felt she belonged.

"When I bought my house here, my small group came over on a Sunday morning—because we're all Saturday night churchgoers—and helped me pack and move. We're family."

Though people may attend church regularly, they might still feel something is missing. They long for a sense of belonging and connection. Small groups can provide that. My husband, Jeff, as mentioned earlier, is the pastor of Small Groups and Discipleship at Northgate Christian Fellowship, and he recognizes the importance of small groups and how they benefit people like Renee and Lani.

One of his responsibilities is to build and shepherd small groups. When he first joined Northgate, weekly attendance was nearing 500, however, the church had only seven small groups. He began exploring ideas for launching new groups. He decided to try his hand at launching a Connection, an idea borrowed from its developer church, Saddleback, in Lake Forest, California.[4]

After getting to know Lani and Renee, Jeff asked their help in getting more small groups on their feet. He gave them a quick sketch of his plan, and Lani and Renee agreed to help. Neither, Jeff, Lani, nor Renee had previous experience with such an event.

Lani had managed the new employee program at Chevron-Texaco. Jeff had already seen her skills in action at their church's new friends' luncheon, designed to help new church attendees learn more about Northgate. Lani enjoyed helping people assimilate and asked herself, "How can I take that and do that for God?"

Most of the ins and outs of how to organize and run the Connection had already been mapped out by Saddleback Church. The Connection provided an environment where those not presently in small groups could connect with one. The event also pinpointed new group leaders to help launch new groups.

Lani and Renee kicked off the event with an icebreaker called human bingo. They gave participants handouts with questions such as "Do you sing in the shower?" or "Do you drive more than 10 miles to church?" The questions were printed in boxes arranged like a Bingo game card, with one question per box. Each participant was to find persons who fit the descriptions in the boxes and get them to sign the boxes they matched. The first person to get a row or column of squares signed on his or her card yelled, "Bingo."

The Connection, in addition to connecting people with groups and culling new leaders, gave church members the opportunity to get to know other church attendees in a relaxed environment. As human bingo unfolded, people found people with whom they had something in common.

Lani and Renee used these common factors from the bingo sheet to gather people together at the end of the game. They called out one of the bingo qualifiers such as "loves dogs" and asked those who had signed that square to gather together.

Similar affinities were used to convene other groups. Groups that were too large (more than 12 members) were narrowed down again after the facilitators selected another qualifier. Though these common threads were somewhat superficial—such as liking the same music or living on the same street—they were connecting points nonetheless.

The biggest surprise came with the process of choosing a leader for each group. The Connection format includes a short Bible lesson taught by one of the Connection facilitators. The facilitator presides over the gathering to give people a taste of what might be studied at a small group. Following this lesson, while people are clustered at tables (again, by like interests determined by the bingo game) a discussion time follows.

Facilitators did not appoint any table leaders to manage the discussion, so chaos reigned at first. This was no accident. It was done to flush out natural facilitators who tend to take charge and facilitate discussion. Following this, a Connection leader asked each table to pray silently about the person they would trust and in whom they would have confidence to lead them in a small group.

When they finished praying, the Connection facilitator counted to three and asked everyone to point to that person. Groups then affirmed the person or persons they picked and why they chose them. Potential leaders were asked to lead small groups composed of members at their table. The commitment would be for approximately two months, after which they would be free to either disband the group or keep going. Connection facilitators met with and coached these new leaders to help prepare them for facilitating the new groups.

Jeff observes, "It amazed me to see those chosen were so willing to take on the task of leading the group."

The outcome of the Connection at Northgate resulted in the launch of 5 new groups. The number of groups went from 7 to 12 groups, a 35 percent increase. Since their first Connection experiment, Northgate has held another, with similar results. Leadership foresees holding it on a semiannual basis as a way to continue launching new groups.

Ice Cream Social Promo

After holding a couple of small-group Connections, Northgate Church leaders mulled over new ways to promote and launch more small groups at church. The Connection succeeded in launching new groups, but not all groups that formed stayed active. Putting groups together that had substantial common interest using the Connection was challenging.

Human bingo provided a few surface connections that weren't as deep as those provided by affinity groups. Recognizing this, leaders arrived at a new idea for launching and promoting groups. Why not have an ice cream social kickoff in the fall? The church borrowed a slogan idea from a well-known ice cream company and promoted the event as "The many flavors of small groups."

The evening began with icebreaker games to help people become acquainted. Following this, visitors were encouraged to visit the festive tables around the room. These were manned by representatives from each small group. Group members were responsible for decorating their tables using their own creative designs. Groups also provided ice cream and toppings (their choice of flavor), as well as flyers that told about their groups. Group representatives talked to visitors about their group while dishing out the ice cream.

The event proved highly successful in launching many new small groups and gaining additional members for existing ones.

Small-Group Ministry Fairs

Ministry fairs are another way to promote small groups. Set up tables in a high traffic area such as the church lobby. Designate tables by ministry category such as care and benevolence, worship arts, and so forth. Make your table displays eye-catching with colorful flyers. Clear plastic sign holders that stand upright are great for designating what ministry area the table falls under. Make sure flyers have contact info such as the ministry purpose, who oversees the ministry, and how to contact them.

A ministry fair can connect people with ministry opportunities but can also be used to highlight small groups as one of your ministry focuses. Consider having a special table just for small groups, with a flyer on each group explaining its purpose.

If you don't want to have an all-out ministry fair, holding one for small groups only might be a solution. As with the regular ministry fair, have flyers for each group that include the group's purpose, where it meets, what the group studies, and who to contact. You can leave tables unattended. However, they seem to be more successful when there is someone behind them to talk with prospects and answer questions.

Make flyers colorful and bright. You have several options. You can have a flyer that lists all of your small groups, a brief one- to two-sentence statement about the group, and contact information for those who are interested in getting involved, or you can have separate flyers for each group. Allowing each group to have a separate flyer gives groups more room to promote themselves with greater detail about what they are all about. At our church, each group is responsible for creating and maintaining their own promotional flyers. Small-group promotional events are most effective when held no more than once or twice a year.

In addition to the ministry fairs and special small-group promotional events, you might want to experiment with a publicity table that features a specific ministry every couple of months. One month the table might promote a specific mission event; another month it might promote small groups. The trick is not to leave the information out all the time. When something is always on display, it eventually becomes invisible. People become so used to seeing it that they no longer notice it. You can solve this challenge by periodically removing the table and/or its contents for a while. Then resurrect it again when enough time has passed.

At the end of this chapter you will see examples of small-group flyers designed to promote a variety of small groups. These may give you some ideas. One of the flyers included at the end of this chapter is one used by the Metamorphosis group mentioned earlier. Note that their info sheet includes not only a mission statement but also core values, which gives potential new group members a good idea of what the group interest and purpose is.

The sheet also includes important group contact information so that potential new members can ask questions and become connected. Consider including a photo of the group contact person. When people know what a leader looks like, they find it easier to connect with him or her face-to-face. The sample flyers on the next few pages are close to the original formats designed by actual groups so that you can see how different groups chose to promote themselves. Feel free to borrow from content, wording, and layout to create your own promotional flyers.

Colorful paper, graphics, and contrasting fonts all help grab the attention of prospective new members. Information you'll want to provide on the flyers includes the group's name, where it meets, when it meets, the group's purpose, what the group is studying, who the leader is, and how to contact him or her.

Here is a sample flyer that used a half sheet of paper on plain white stock.

Northgate Christian Single Parent Support Group

We offer helpful information and guidance on stress management, blending families, boundaries, dating, power of prayer, divorce recovery, and coping with the challenges of single parenting. We are here to try and meet the needs of single parents.

> He comforts us in all our troubles so that we can comfort others. When they are troubled, we will be able to give them the same comfort God has given us (2 Cor. 1:4, NLT).

We meet second and fourth Tuesdays 6:30–7:30 P.M. at the church.

Our Mission Statement: Our purpose is to serve the single parent community so that they might:
- Engage in a personal relationship with God
- Nurture their children in love and discipline
- Encourage one another to grow spiritually, emotionally, and socially

Youth room available for children's activities.

It's the group that makes it happen. Call anytime if you have questions or concerns.

Group Leader: [Name] [phone number] [E-mail address]

This is the flyer for the Metamorphosis group, which was mentioned in this chapter and chapter 3.

METAMORPHOSIS
GROUP PURPOSE & FOCUS
Metamorphosis has a twofold purpose:

1. Maturity—to grow and mentor Christ followers to become mature Christians, using God's Word as adviser and compass.

2. Ministry—to develop, equip, and encourage the leader in every believer so that he or she can bring others into a mature relationship with Christ.

Core Values

- We love stretching and growing, so we share teaching and hosting responsibilities and we sometimes take on projects so we can reach out to others in ministry.

- We love fun, so we have frequent fun types of events and gatherings.

- We love food, so eating and fellowship are a big part of this group.

- We value learning biblical principles to apply to our daily lives.

- We love supporting each other, so we share prayer requests and concerns because we see each other as family.

When Do We Meet? Every other Thursday night in different group members' homes. Start time 6:45 P.M. Stop time 8:45 P.M.

Child Care Provided? Child care is up to each particular group member although several of our members collaborate from time to time.

Photo	CONTACT INFO
	[Name]
	[Phone Number]
	[E-mail address]

Here is an example of a group that matched their name to their study.

ROAMIN' THROUGH ROMANS

TUES. OCT. 5, 7 P.M.
STARTS:

WHERE: [Address]

LEADERS: [Name(s)] [Phone number(s)]

WHO: YOUNG ADULTS THROUGH THEIR 30S. AFTER
           THAT YOUNG TAKES ON A NEW MEANING . . .
           (WE KNOW)

WHAT: INSIGHTS FROM PAUL'S RELEVANT BOOK OF
           ROMANS, SHOWING US HOW TO HAVE A LIFE
           RICH IN PURPOSE AND STRONG WITH LOVE

DESSERT PROVIDED

REMEMBER ALL THOSE COOKIES FROM THE MEXICO
MISSION COOKIE SALES?

Page 1 of outside of Northgate Christian Fellowship's Celebrate Recovery brochure. This is a trifold brochure.

CELEBRATE RECOVERY

Northgate Christian Fellowship

address

phone

e-mail

NORTH GATE
CHRISTIAN FELLOWSHIP

Tools for Living Life with Peace and Joy

Current Class

The Truth Shall Set You Free

- Are you living in a treadmill existence?
- Do you constantly try to please others and achieve unrealistic goals?
- Do you have a sense of incompleteness and feel compelled to seek something better?
- Do you wonder that no matter how hard you try, things don't change?

Mondays 6:30 P.M. at Northgate

Leader: [Name]
[Phone number]

For future classes call Mike for schedule

Chemical Dependency . . . .

- Do you drink or use drugs to escape life?
- Do your loved ones constantly ask you to quit using or to seek help?
- Are your relationships in turmoil or deteriorating?
- Do you find yourself thinking about your next drink or how you can get your drugs?

Mondays 6:30 P.M. at Northgate

Leader: [Name]
[Phone number]

Page 2 of inside of Northgate's Celebrate Recovery brochure.

Codependency . . .

- Do you feel compelled to help solve others' problems?

- Is your attention focused on other's needs and desires?

- Are you loyal, remaining in harmful relationships or situations too long?

- Do you try to control events and influence others' behaviors?

Sundays 6:30 P.M. at Northgate

Leader: [Name]
[Phone number]

Eating Disorders . . .

- Do thoughts about food occupy much of your time?

- Are you preoccupied with the desire to be thinner?

- Have you tried to diet repeatedly, only to sabotage your weight loss?

- Do you eat even when you are not hungry?

Mondays 6:30 P.M.

Leader: [Name]
[Phone number]

For anyone struggling with hurts, habits, or hang-ups . . . that have you stuck in behaviors that keep you from experiencing the fullness and joy in life . . . .

At some point, everyone can use a little help getting unstuck.

We can help!

The small groups who created these two separate flyers used half sheets of paper.

Flyer 1—Christian Educators in Prayer

Christian Educators in Prayer

Pray for students

Pray for parents

Pray for school

Pray for our communities

Pray with us on the first Thursday each month

From 7 to 8 P.M.

At Northgate Church

For more information call [Name] [Phone Number]

Flyer 2—Praise and Worship Bible Study

*Our Thursday night Bible study is a group of imperfect people
striving to do God's perfect will. We believe that the group
is there for the members. It is a relaxing atmosphere where
you do not have to feel bad when you cannot make it or have
to leave early. You only participate or read when you want to.
We start out each week with our greetings, then sing three
to four songs of praise and worship. We then do our
Bible study. The booklet we are currently using is
"James: A Faith That Works." We close with praise
and prayer requests. We try to follow
where the Spirit leads us.*

*Our hostess, Lee, makes everyone feel very welcome
by opening her home and always having
a wonderful spread of snack foods.*

*We would love to have you in our group. If not, please join
another. They are great places of love and growth.*

We meet Thursdays at 7 P.M. at [address].
[Phone number]
Leader: [Name] [Phone Number]

Flyers like this one and the next can be created easily using clip art and/or stylish typefaces.

Wednesday Night Small Group

WHERE: [Address and phone number]

TIME: 7:30 P.M. every Wednesday night

WHY: To fellowship and discuss the Bible

Please come and join our small group, which meets every Wednesday night. We review Pastor Ken's or Pastor Jeff's Sunday sermon message outline and discuss how it applies to our daily lives. We enjoy praying together and studying the Bible, but our main focus is to have fellowship with our Christian brothers and sisters.

Current Group Members
[Names, addresses, and phone numbers]

Exodus

A Nice Place to Visit, but . . .

We invite you to join us for Bible facts (verse by verse), food, and fellowship as we journey from Egypt toward Mount Sinai with the Israelites.

In addition to our time in God's Word, we have outside activities that include picnics, baseball games, and movies!

Tuesdays at 7:30 P.M.
We are traveling like the Israelites
So call to find out this week's address
See you this coming Tuesday?

Contact [Name(s)] [Phone number(s)]

The "flyer" for the Cholesterol Café was run off on a full sheet of paper and folded into quarters much like a greeting card. The paper used was a bright, eye-catching yellow.

Back Cover

Front Cover

It's as Crazy as It Sounds!

Cholesterol Café

Men's Prayer Breakfast

Inside Left

Inside Right

TED WILLIAMS' 83-YEAR-OLD BODY WAS FROZEN AT -320°F

Why do you call me good? . . . No one is good— except God alone (Mark 10:18).

Every Friday Morning

6 A.M.

WAFFLE IRON on Highway 10

As you can see, the flyers developed for the ministry fair are a wonderful way to display the variety and uniqueness of small groups. I had the opportunity to talk with a pastor of small groups and assimilation. He not only oversees the spiritual development of members but also is in charge of coaching and launching small groups. One of the areas in which many churches struggle is in finding ways to get people connected quickly. A solution to this problem might be found in what this pastor is doing.

His church has a series of foundational classes for its members. First in this series is a class called First Step. First Step is a membership class that explains not only what the church believes but also how to make a commitment to Christ. Occasionally attendees hear the plan of salvation and make a profession of faith.

Concerned that these young Christians might not get the nurture they needed in their newfound faith, the pastor toyed with launching a small group from First Step graduates at the conclusion of each class. His hope was that by making this immediate connection with new members, the graduates would become a part of this smaller, intimate fellowship. Such a group would then provide maturity and biblical training and increase the likelihood that they would continue to attend the church because of a sense of connectedness.

It's too early to know if this idea worked, but I applaud the pastor for trying. As leaders we should always be looking for new ways to assimilate members so that they grow in Christian maturity. Small groups are a crucial part of that process.

Points to Ponder
Identifying Potential Small-Group Leaders

If your church has small groups already in place, ask group leaders to complete the form below. If small groups are not in place, have some of your church leaders complete the form. This information can help you identify potential small-group leaders. Where each blank appears, fill in the name or names of people who come to mind who might become leader apprentices.

_____ rarely misses meetings.

_____ often shares wise spiritual insights.

_____ is respected among group members.

_____ shows signs of being a mature Christian.

_____ cares about the general welfare of group members.

_____ sometimes takes on a leadership role when help is needed or asked.

_____ would possibly take on leadership responsibility if asked.

_____ is biblically grounded (familiar with Scripture and applies it to his or her life).

_____ seems to sincerely care about the spiritual and physical well-being of group members.

_____ might have the time to commit to facilitating a small group.

_____ has previously taught lessons either in a small-group setting or in a church classroom setting.

5   a diversity of small groups

Few things have changed my life like the small groups
I have been in over the last 30 years.
Currently I'm in two—
a leader's discipleship group and,
for 25 years, a weekly one-on-one meeting
for fellowship and prayer. The most intense learning,
growth, sharing, encouragement, accountability,
prayer, and fellowship I've experienced have
taken place in small groups.
—Patrick Morley[1]

Human struggles with addictions, substance abuse, codependency, and broken-ness are centuries old. When life gets tough, people look for ways to dull the pain. Their coping methods may provide a temporary reprieve, but these often develop long-term destructive patterns. Peoples' choices affect them as well as those around them. Often these unhealthy lifestyles and coping methods pass from one generation to the next. This creates more situations where there is substance abuse, fractured relationships, and deep, long-lasting wounds.

Saddleback Church in Lake Forest, California, has always been on the cut-ting edge of church ministry. Their recovery groups program is one example. The church deliberately reaches outside the confines of traditional church ministry and targets seekers—those on the fringes who might not otherwise attend church.

Even in its youth, Saddleback used innovative processes to reach out. Some-times attempts at fresh approaches worked well and sometimes they didn't. De-spite some failed efforts, the church still had a strong impact on the surround-ing community. Many came to Christ.

As more and more hurting people walked through Saddleback's doors, their growth exploded. Key leaders recognized the need to develop more effec-tive ways to minister to the hurting. Though many people were committing their lives to Christ, they entered their relationship with Jesus amid brokenness and pain. Hurts brought with them included divorce, drug addiction, alcoholism, and even sexual abuse.

A Sunday sermon alone wasn't enough to heal the deep wounds, and though Saddleback had many small groups in place, existing groups were not equipped to deal with these types of issues. Pastor John Baker, the church's pastor of Recovery and Small Groups, himself a recovering alcoholic, understood the recovery process firsthand, and he developed a program that would minister to these needs.

As observed earlier, Celebrate Recovery was based on the Alcoholics Anonymous 12-step program; it was Christ-centered and fellowship-centered. People gathered not only to learn about Christ but also to talk about their wounds and act as encouragers and accountability partners for each other.

Recovery Groups: Helping Hurting People

Your church need not be the size of Saddleback to develop an effective recovery ministry. Many churches of different sizes have launched effective recovery ministries and have seen them rapidly expand to meet deep needs.

Recovery groups bring longtime and in-depth healing. Group participants learn that despite their bad choices, their new life in Christ gives them the freedom to start over. They may still have to deal with poor choices of the past, but do so with hope of overcoming. Such groups are also a way of bridging the gap into the community.

Many hurting people would never dream of coming to a church. Their own brokenness and fear of what others might think or how they will react holds them back. Churches that provide a grace shelter where wounded people can come and be healed draw in many who would not otherwise have entered the church doors. Once the word gets out that a church is a healing church, barriers start to come down. Dependents and codependents from within the church body and community come to these groups for healing.

Recovery programs such as Celebrate Recovery are not just for alcoholics or substance abusers. They also minister to individuals and their families. Groups address a variety of needs, including codependent relationships, eating disorders, failure to bond in relationships, how to set healthy boundaries, smoking addictions, sexual and physical abuse, adult children of alcoholics, sexual and relationship addictions, and in some cases even posttraumatic stress syndrome.

Jeff Van Vonderen, author of *Good News for the Chemically Dependent and Those Who Love Them*,[2] is an intervention specialist, a speaker, and consultant on addiction, family systems, and recovery. He recognizes that support for chemically dependent people within the church body is rare. VanVonderen's goal is to teach families of the chemically dependent how to respond to them. He also hopes to enlighten Christians, Christian counselors, and clergy regarding how to improve their responses to individuals and families torn apart by these destructive circumstances.

The church body often plays the shame game, shaming the dependent person by stressing the law rather than grace. Many Christ followers might agree that problems of alcohol, drugs, or other destructive and addictive behaviors are not talked about except in a negative way because those habits and behaviors are viewed as sinful. The stigma and shame associated with dependency has several effects.

Dependents may steer away from church because they feel judged. Or they may put on a false front of having reformed. Some conversions may be genuine. But even if they enter a relationship with Christ, the original cause of the dependency—which is accompanied often by poor self-image and/or deep wounds—still remains. In addition, families who have had to live with this dysfunction at length are suddenly left trying to readjust how they interact with this person.

Committing one's life to Christ does not end all struggles, because unhealthy behaviors are so deeply rooted in both the former dependent and his or her loved ones. Former dependents may develop new healthier patterns or turn back to old ways for comfort. In order for the transformation to stick, they must replace old behaviors with new, healthier ones. This is where recovery groups come in.

Recovery groups provide support that helps these individuals and their hurting family members recover. When drastic changes are needed, people progress fastest when they have support from people other than just their family. These are those with whom they build trust and to whom they become accountable. A network of caring people for those in recovery can make a huge difference. Fortifying this network with a scriptural foundation provides needed guidelines and wisdom.

In order for recovery to happen, both the dependent and codependent must take steps to become healthy. "Shhh. We don't talk about that" seems to be the historical stand the church has taken. VanVonderen urges churches to bring recovery issues into the open and work at becoming God-based, grace-filled environments where people can experience forgiveness and healing.

To effectively promote healing and wholeness of members, churches need to acknowledge these issues and promote resources and programs to deal with them in a positive way. One of the first steps is to allow members to look at recovery programs and how they function. The more they know about such programs and their foundational principles, the better they will understand the issues and challenges facing those in recovery.

•——— ———◀

Several church leaders milled about their church's lobby waiting for the service to end. They talked about the spring weather and how the early spring affected people's allergies. Dave,* a recovering alcoholic and active church member, said, "I don't take cold or allergy medicines anymore. It's just too risky. You know my history. I don't want to take any chances on going back to my old ways."

The other leaders looked thoughtful. Dave had come to Christ a few years earlier. Before he became a Christ follower he sometimes abused medications along with alcohol. He depended on his recovery group for the support and courage he needed to stay clean and sober. His recovery history included overcoming the temptation of abusing other substances.

Many former dependents face Dave's types of struggles every day. But unlike Dave, they would probably never feel free to share what he had with other church leaders. Because Dave's church supported recovery, other members did as well. Through this safe environment they enabled Dave to find his way back to wholeness.

•——— ———◀

Birthing Recovery Groups

A growing church stretched its pastors to oversee multiple duties. More and more people needed counseling. Those in need might benefit from a support venue where they could talk about their problems and perhaps gain encouragement and insight from others. Issues ranged from domestic violence to threat of divorce. The pastoral staff recognized the unlikelihood that they could continue to do all of the counseling. Perhaps lay counseling and support groups were the answer.

One pastor worked with Darin* to help him launch a recovery program. Darin, a divorced recovering alcoholic, had come to Christ after going through some difficult life circumstances. Together the pastor and Darin attended a recovery training seminar. Upon their return they worked to develop a recovery program and promote and announce the first meeting. The new concept was foreign to most church members. Clear explanations and repetitious promotion helped people grasp what it was about.

─────────

*Not their real names.

Soon Darin enlisted other ambassadors, people in recovery, to help promote the program. They talked to people they knew who might benefit from the ministry. After several months of preparation, studying the curriculum, and promoting the group, they had a cookout to launch the program. Following the meal everyone gathered to hear more about the group and its purpose. A guest speaker shared about his own recovery process.

In just two years' time the church birthed five recovery groups with the promise of many more. One is for divorce recovery, one is for teens in families of chemically dependent people, one is for those recovering from chemical dependency, one is for eating disorders, and a new one is for adult codependents.

Today the church's recovery participants grow in their relationships with Christ while helping each other overcome their deep wounds. Their stories are both painful and joyful as group members more fully understand Christ's love and grace. Though the recovery program hasn't eliminated the need for pastoral counseling or lay counseling, it has certainly lightened the pastor's load.

How do counseling and recovery groups differ? Counseling usually happens with a counselor and one or two people. Recovery groups work in a small-group setting. Most often groups study a lesson, watch a DVD, or both. A group facilitator then leads groups through questions and a sharing time, where much of the healing takes place. People learn to identify their work areas by talking about the lesson and reflecting on their lives. Through sharing and encouragement from the facilitator and fellow group members, they, in a sense, learn to be their own counselors.

The more a church attempts to reach unchurched people, the greater the need for recovery programs and lay-counseling programs. Churches, and the people they serve, benefit from developing proactive rather than reactive resources and support groups. Rather than deal with the aftermath of bad choices, creating programs to curb and teach about destructive behaviors can actually prevent brokenness.

A small group on parenting or one dedicated to teaching strong marriage relationships might be on the front end of a church's labors and could be developed either through recovery programs or lay counseling programs. Such resources reduce the problems that arise. A lack of these resources often results in an increase in strained marital relationships or parenting crises. Imagine the improvements in the relationships and life skills of congregational members that will come from establishing groups to help equip them for success in these important matters.

Our lay-counseling group takes strong measures to protect both its counselors and clients. After training and before entering into counseling, all facilitators sign a clause, which guarantees client/counselor confidentiality. In addition, once a counselee reviews and completes an initial counseling question-naire, both the client and the counselor sign an agreement. The purpose of this agreement is to enforce an accountability standard between the facilitators and participants and to ensure that each party understands how the program oper-ates and what his or her role will be.

Churches today face increased liabilities. Having recovery group facilitators and participants sign an agreement summarizing how the program will operate can prevent misunderstandings and underscore the "rules." Doing this verifies to all involved that facilitators are not licensed counselors and will not be acting as such. Also, this practice ensures that all are aware of the agreement's confiden-tiality clause. With such safeguards in place churches decrease the chances of le-gal issues that might later arise.

Signed agreements need not be mandatory; however, they can act as a safe-ty buffer while bringing clarity about conduct and operations to all involved. You'll find sample agreements in the appendix should you wish to use them. You can easily adapt these for your own program's needs.

When Should You Start?

When should you start a recovery program? Begin by looking at your church's climate and current needs. Launching a program without making sure the need exists wastes time and human resources. Avoid the pitfall of starting a program and finding someone to run it. Look for signs of life first. If recovery needs are apparent—for instance, if your paid staff is spending more and more time in counseling situations with deeply hurting people—then you've already got a pulse.

Recovery might be a future focus. Pray for God to raise up leaders with the passion to meet those needs. Like John Walker and Jeff VanVonderen, many Christians have a recovery story to tell. Screen potential recovery leaders care-fully. Most will have a past. These are exactly the kinds of people God wants to use. Look for solid, healthy Christians who show signs of working toward ma-turity and stability. Though they are in the process of becoming what God wants them to be (just as we all are), God will use them in amazing ways.

One way to determine if a need for recovery exists in your church while flushing out potential leaders is by scheduling a forum where people can talk about tough issues, such as chemical dependency. At one former church where I served, I held a special forum on depression. Having struggled with depres-sion myself, I recognized the struggle in others. I invited a licensed Christian counselor to come and speak on the subject. We had an excellent turnout. I had no idea that depression affected the lives of so many. Some wrestled with it themselves; others had family members who struggled. The interest shown proved that often the needs are bubbling below the surface.

Just as depression issues are rarely talked about in church, so, too, are dependency issues. Van Vonderen's church held a similar forum. They scheduled four Sunday evening sessions called Breaking the Silence: Beginning to Deal with Tough Issues. Then they invited experts on the subjects they presented at the sessions. Topics covered included protecting children from sexual abuse, family violence, and shame. Their format provided information and resources for both professional counselors and laypeople, and as VanVonderen stressed, it emphasized that the issues were *our* issues not *their* issues.[3]

Here is just one example. A couple who had recently committed their lives to Christ belonged to a small group. Both husband and wife were excited about learning more about God's Word and growing their faith. Unfortunately, the sudden hospitalization of the husband's father required him to leave town to be with him. For a while it looked as if the father might not pull through.

The trip home, back to his roots, brought this young man back into contact with his extremely dysfunctional family. The past included an alcoholic parent, sexual abuse by a "friend" of the family, incarceration of the father, and a false accusation brought by a sibling who accused this young man of trying to manipulate and cheat his father out of the will while he lay gravely ill.

These events caused suppressed memories to resurface, and suddenly this young Christian man began to have serious health issues brought on by the stress of the situation. He could no longer cope, largely due to the dysfunction and wounds caused by his extended family.

Stories of similar family dysfunction are becoming more and more common. Church ministry work puts ministry leaders in touch with those with painful pasts, which include physical, emotional, and sexual abuse; abortions, alcoholism, and more. I know one individual who before coming to Christ used drugs so heavily that at one point he lived in a shack with no water or electricity. Today John has a wonderful Christian testimony. Individuals like John have found support in the church. Many share their stories with others. They recognize they need specialized groups related to their own personal struggles to help them overcome and become healthy once again.

The battle with these and other issues is lifelong. Only through a strong group support network do most people stay reformed, because the temptation to fall back into the old way of coping with the pain is ever present. Holding forums or classes such as the one VanVonderen's church held gives people permission to look at these matters in a new light. If you hold such a forum, you may be surprised at the deep needs that surface. God will raise the leaders you need to make recovery support groups possible.

Healing People from the Inside Out

To have an impact on their world, churches must try to stay culturally relevant. Those who don't usually end up internally focused, trying to maintain existing programs that cater to the social club mentality of long-standing members. Just because you have always done ministry a certain way doesn't mean it should continue that way. Recovery groups may sound like just one more gimmick to try in order to tap into the latest trend, but they go much deeper. They meet an earnest need for healing and wholeness.

Recovery groups often extend their reach outside their church walls. Some advertise in the community section of local newspapers, where club activities are promoted. External focus is admirable, but be aware that individuals who come may bring their quirks with them. They may not be Christ followers. Equip your church body to connect with them.

Be ready to share the Christian message without the Christianese church lingo. When the message of Christ is made understandable, more people will seize the opportunity to commit their lives to Him. The first priority is to provide a safe haven for hurting people by extending grace. On the back end, churches can work to bring them into a relationship with Christ.

Some of the more tenured members in your church body may feel squeamish about the types of people who show up at your doors once a recovery program is underway. You can reduce the resistance by educating members about the importance of the recovery program and showing them how lives are being changed.

One of the most powerful ways your church can educate its members about recovery is by allowing recovery participants to share their stories of brokenness and healing with them. Some churches do this on occasion during worship services, through live interviews or recorded videos. Nothing speaks louder than the personal, sincere testimony of someone who has entered a relationship with Christ from a recovery standpoint.

When churches learn to tune into the hurts and needs of the body rather than trying to ignore the needs and hope they go away, they open the door to true healing. The impact can be far-reaching, from generation to generation.

Affinity Groups: Specialized Small Groups

A few years ago Jack Canfield, a well-known motivational speaker, generated an idea for a book called *Chicken Soup for the Soul*. The book is a compilation of inspirational stories of real people. Mr. Canfield had no idea he was unleashing a publisher's dream. The book started a phenomenal chain reaction of successive spin-off books.

The momentum is still going today as hundreds of *Chicken Soup for the Soul* titles target specific niches. They include books like *Chicken Soup for the Teacher's Soul, Chicken Soup for the Camper's Soul, Chicken Soup for the Grandparent's Soul,* and many more. The possibilities seem endless, and though we may want to throw our hands in the air and say, "Enough," one thing is clear. Mr. Canfield scratched an itch—obviously a very large one. People could not get enough of the Chicken Soup books.

The books are similar to affinity groups because they cover topics that draw the attention of specific individuals with common interests in the same subject matter. Affinity groups scratch a shared itch. Like the Chicken Soup books, affinity groups start with generic interests. Something as simple as people wanting to study the Bible and fellowship together can be a starting point.

Such interest covers a broad range of people, since singles, young people, married couples, and so on, all may have similar interests. But if you narrow the group focus to more specific needs, interests, and even demographics, you'll increase your impact.

Effective affinity groups meet the specific needs of individuals based on their interests and life journeys. They provide an environment where like-minded people gather and share common interests that in time bind them together into a tight, caring, family-like relationship.

Affinity groups provide not only an opportunity for Christians to grow and receive nourishment but also an environment where non-Christians can come and learn more about Christ. Common interests draw people together and lead to common ground, and eventually, in some cases, provide a bridge to sharing the gospel with individuals who may not otherwise be open to hearing the story.

So affinity groups can be helpful for almost anyone. Non-Christians as well as Christians can find nurture, care, and support in an affinity group. What's more, the kinds of groups that can be formed are many and varied. Just about any interest can be the focus of a group. Here are just a few ideas for possible affinity groups.

Biblical foundations groups. Some churches call these Bible basic groups or faith journey groups. The purpose of these groups is to offer basic spiritual and scriptural training and deepen the faith and spiritual foundations of new believers.

Sports groups. Bowling, hiking, camping, chess, soccer, baseball, fishing, rock climbing, roller hockey, volleyball, basketball, hunting, boating, swimming, wrestling, umpiring, coaching, and so on—almost any sport can be the interest of an affinity group.

Recovery/support groups. Divorce, substance abuse, physical abuse, grief, weight issues, eating disorders, anger management, depression, and so on, are all issues with which people wrestle, and each or all can be the focus of an affinity group.

Parenting. Parents of preschoolers, parents of teens, parents of children with special needs, moms' groups, grandparents raising grandchildren, adoptive parents, blended families—many people need not only parenting skills but also fellowship and the opportunity to share parenting knowledge and issues with other parents.

Singles. Divorce recovery, single moms, single dads, college and career age participants, and so on—there are so many different types of singles, and lumping all singles into one group rarely creates an effective affinity group. Singles groups work best when they focus on a specific type of singleness.

Marriage. Marriage support and marriage strengthening, young married couples, seasoned married couples, marriage mentors (the paring up of oldyweds with newlyweds), second time around marriages (for those who have remarried) . . .

Business and professionals. Entrepreneurs, writers, medical professionals, Realtors . . .

Arts and crafts. Scrapbooking, quilting, ceramics, drawing, painting, carving, sewing . . .

Music. Learning to play guitar, music appreciation, worship team small groups . . .

Benevolence. Food pantries, soup kitchens, community service, general benevolence . . .

Leader groups. Church leaders, business leaders, mentoring leaders, children's leaders, youth leaders . . .

Women's groups. Single women, young married women, widows, divorcés, women in business . . .

Men's groups. Single men, young married men, widowers, divorcés . . .

Teens' groups. Teen boys, teen girls, middle school teens, high school teens, troubled teens, at risk teens, teens of parents in recovery . . .

Miscellaneous. Retirees, financial management, evangelism, missions . . .

As you can see, there are countless types of affinity groups. The possibilities are endless.

The Key to Successful Affinity Groups

People are more open to learning Christian principles when they see Christ reflected in the lives of the group leader and Christians within the group. Affinity group leaders may intend for their groups to have a spiritual emphasis.

The challenge, however, is to balance fun with spirituality so that the group doesn't merely become a social club. One way to maintain this balance is to develop a mission statement, core values, and a group covenant.

When establishing a small group, keep the following in mind:

- Allow ample time for sharing, in which members can be honest about their struggles.
- Plan social outings where group members can simply have fun.
- Plan outreach projects that reflect shared interests and stretch group members. Doing so will keep the group from becoming too inwardly focused.
- Be alert to those whose interests and issues make them a good fit for the group.
- When inviting new people to join the group, explain the group's target audience, purpose, and topic of study.

Points to Ponder
Is Your Church Facilitating Recovery?

1. Does your church have any recovery groups?

2. Who do you know who has suffered from the effects of chemical dependency either directly as a user or indirectly as a codependent?

3. What individuals in your church might be strong advocates of a recovery group?

   Why?

4. If your church doesn't currently have any types of recovery groups in place, what could be done to start them?

5. Have you been affected either directly or indirectly by some type of recovery issue, such as alcohol abuse, drug abuse, eating disorder, physical abuse, sex abuse, divorce, workaholism, or something other?

What does this tell you about the importance of recovery groups?

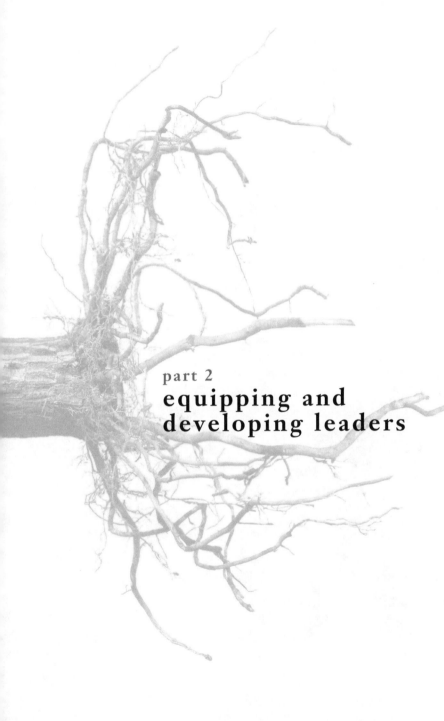

part 2
**equipping and
developing leaders**

6 are you training or straining your leaders?

> Small groups provide the "pond" for what we call the
> "lily pad" of leadership development. People go from
> one lily pad of development to the next.
> Every member is not only a minister;
> every member must also be a multiplier.
> —Brett Eastman[1]

Our daughter, Rachel, teaches high school English and spent four years preparing for teaching. She took classes in language and teaching skills and spent time in the classroom getting hands-on experience. Though she has always been a mature young woman, and despite the training she received, her inexperience showed when she began her first year of teaching. She learned quickly that teaching was filled with all sorts of interesting challenges.

My friend Sue, a middle school principal, says she can usually tell after meeting with a new teacher whether he or she will remain in that profession after three years. By the end of their third year, most novice teachers have decided whether they will continue as teachers or switch to another vocation.

Some find they are exactly where they are supposed to be, while others decide they aren't wired for teaching after all. (I doubt I would last six months as a teacher after having seen the difficulty of their jobs.) Teachers who stick it out must surely love what they do.

Why Train Leaders?

Just as novice schoolteachers go through a screening process to learn if they are suited for teaching, novice small-group leaders may also go through a filtering process. Some dive confidently into leadership. Others may be unsure of themselves. Even though some individuals seem like naturals for leading a small group, small-group-leader training can increase their success. Leader training lays a strong foundation by improving a leader's ability to respond successfully to challenges that arise while shepherding.

A church scheduled equipping sessions for its small-group leaders. Though the leadership did not make these meetings mandatory, small-group leaders were strongly urged to attend. The church held training sessions for half a day on Saturdays and covered:

- Group covenants and guidelines plus how to use them
- How to develop healthy, balanced small groups that share responsibilities
- How to use auxiliary materials for teaching a Bible study, such as concordances, Bible dictionaries, and Bible reference books
- Recommended Bible study materials for use in group study
- Having group leaders share about their group, its purpose, and meeting times
- Opportunities where leaders could talk about challenges they faced as group leaders

First-time leaders found the training particularly helpful because it gave them guidelines for managing their groups. Providing regular leadership training helps equip leaders and increases the chance of small-group success. The downside of this type of format is that seasoned small-group leaders or those who have previously attended group training may find the information repetitive.

Formal Training

If your church already has small groups, leader experience may vary widely. Some leaders may be moderately experienced. Some may be complete novices who have never led any church ministry before, including small groups. Others may be seasoned leaders with experience in other ministry areas and are taking on group leadership for the first time.

With experience so varied, expertise will be too. New leaders often experience anxiety about how to lead a group. Since small-group leaders have different levels of experience, a special training session covering the basics just for new leaders is often beneficial.

Veteran leaders have different concerns and needs. You don't want to put them through the same training sessions as newer, less experienced leaders. Even with separate training opportunities, you can still train all ranges of leaders on the same day. One way of dealing with this diversity of experience is to divide leaders into novice leaders and seasoned leaders.

Hold a training session for first-time leaders earlier in the day and a session for practiced leaders following. Between the first session and the second session, you might sandwich a sharing and networking session. All leaders can participate in this special session while they get acquainted, network, and share ideas.

Some churches offer quarterly leader training sessions for group leaders. Others only provide something once a year. Still others have no leader training in place. If your church doesn't presently offer training, start laying the groundwork for it. Once training is in place, it's wise to offer ongoing training and mentoring opportunities so leaders can continue to sharpen leadership skills and receive the support they need.

Basic Training for Novice Leaders

Every branch of the armed forces has some form of basic training so that new recruits learn the ropes and disciplines needed for full-time service. Just as boot camp uses seasoned leaders to teach green recruits, you might want to enlist some experienced group leaders to assist with formal training sessions. Leaders like to share what they know, and their knowledge will be invaluable.

Cover mission statements and guidelines. Cover mission statements and guidelines in your beginning leader class. Include information on how to write group guidelines, core values, and optional covenants. Inexperienced leaders often feel most comfortable when they can watch and learn. Provide hands-on examples, such as copies of small-group flyers, sample guidelines, and so on.

Consider giving leaders a template to work from. If time permits, you might even include class time where each leader can work on his or her group's mission statement, guidelines, and core values. The Questions for Establishing the Group Mission Statement, Core Values, and Guidelines listed at the end of chapter 3 will be helpful for this purpose. Copy them and allow class participants to use them as work sheets.

Brainstorm group names. Establishing group names comes next. If you have enough new leaders enrolled in your class, give them a few moments to either brainstorm names together or work on names in their spare time by using the space provided at the bottom of the Questions for Establishing . . . section. Though it's ideal to have a group name before they start promoting their groups, leaders can ask group members to help choose a name.

Have you ever been asked to do something and then found you had sparse instruction on how to do it? No one enjoys volunteering under those conditions, and small-group leaders are no exception. Equipping leaders is a crucial step in developing effective small groups. Below is a brief introduction. The next two chapters take a more in-depth look at equipping leaders, including choosing curriculum and mentoring leaders.

Discuss study material options. No training session for small-group leaders is complete without some discussion on how to choose study materials. As mentioned earlier, it's beneficial to have sample resources of small-group studies available for leaders to look over at trainings sessions. Groups may be at different points when leaders attend your sessions. Some might be just starting a study, while others may be concluding one. Even experienced leaders have difficulty knowing what to study next. The appendix of this book includes a list of potential small-group studies you might want to recommend for both seasoned and novice leaders.

Help them break the ice. Inaugural meetings for small groups can be pretty intimidating, especially if group members don't know each other. Novice leaders can incorporate an icebreaker into their first group meeting to help members get acquainted.

One small group developed an icebreaker for that purpose. The leader distributed a list of 20 questions to each member. These included simple questions such as, "Where were you born?" and more thought-provoking questions such as, "What was the toughest thing about growing up?"

Group members only had to answer 10 out of 20 questions, dropping their questions into a cup. The leader then pulled out and read random questions, asking members to guess who they thought wrote down the answers. The icebreaker helped members get to know each other better. You'll find some recommended icebreaker resources in the appendix.

Every new leader approaches leadership differently. Some dive in with confidence. Some wade in slowly. New leaders often lack assurance, frightened by the responsibility of being in charge of a group. One way to ease their fears is by stressing that they will act more as facilitators than leaders. Assure them that they will have the support of their group members plus a wealth of knowledge and assistance from seasoned leaders. With training and support they can become the best leaders they can be.

Points to Ponder
Easing the Fears of Novice Leaders

When working with new small-group leaders, take note of any fears and reservations they have about leading. Talk with the leaders candidly about their worries. Reassure them that someone is available to answer their questions and assist with any concerns they might have. Provide them with the names and contact information of those who can coach them. (Make sure you get permission from the contact persons first.)

You want leaders to be with you for the long haul. Spending a little extra time addressing their concerns at the beginning prepares them for success and increases the chances that they will continue to lead.

7   coaching and mentoring leaders

No church with more than 50 members can be effective in
pastoral care without enlisting and enabling the lay
people to do [the] daily work of pastoral care.
—Dale Galloway[1]

Shortly after completing a home addition, our new plantation shutters arrived
for our bedroom window. Jeff eagerly read the installation instructions. "Look
at these instructions!" He held out an illustrated sheet. They seemed clear
enough, but upon closer inspection I saw the written directions on the right
side were cut off. So they read something like this.

"1. Remove panels from frame pieces by p--- out hinge.

2. Be sure hanging strips are lev--."

We laughed. Jeff made the best of it and plunged in, filling in the blanks
with his own words where they were missing. But he ran into a new snag,
when he saw that the screws enclosed with the shutters were not typical
screws. Neither a flathead nor Phillips' head screwdriver worked to install the
screws. Jeff rumbled and grumbled around trying different tools in his quest to
install the shutters. None of them worked. Finally, he gave up and went to the
hardware store where he purchased *normal* screws and completed the job
quickly after returning home.

Creating the Right Conditions

What does installing shutters have to do with small groups, you may ask?
Sometimes we either fail to offer our leaders directions or support for getting
the job done or, like the instructions for the shutters, the information we provide is incomplete. We inadvertently set leaders up for failure. Developing effective tools, resources, and methods to help small-group leaders successfully
manage and mentor their groups teaches them how to lead. One of the easiest
things we can do is to create the right conditions under which equipping takes
place naturally.

This may be as simple as scheduling regular gatherings where small-group leaders can get together. Doing so . . .

Provides valuable networking. Learning happens naturally when leaders share information. At our church's small-group leader meeting, one group leader explained that his group wanted to become involved in a monthly mission or outreach project, but the group had no idea how or where to do such a ministry. A leader of one of the other groups immediately connected this member with the church's Benevolence Team and some of its caring ministries.

Allows leaders to share their mission. Group leaders learn the importance of writing out and adhering to a mission for their groups. They also gain an understanding of each group's purpose. They can refer people to these other groups based on needs and interests when they see another group might be a better fit for a prospective group member's needs.

Helps leaders share curriculum and study ideas. One of the toughest challenges for small-group leaders is knowing what to study. Novice leaders are especially unsure of where to find resources. When leaders share what they are studying, other leaders learn about those materials and can consider using them for their own groups.

You might even encourage leaders to write short book reviews of study materials and leadership resources they have found useful. Running off copies of these reviews for leader networking sessions or in the church newsletter or bulletin can be very helpful to others.

Provides troubleshooting input. Gathering leaders together lets them talk about leadership issues they may face pertaining to their group. Sometimes the solution is allowing leaders to see that other leaders have faced and worked their way through similar problems.

Provides encouragement. A schoolteacher started a monthly prayer group to pray for area teachers, schools, and students. During a small-group leader networking session this leader spoke of her discouragement because her group consisted of only five people. Several other leaders at her table felt that five people was an excellent number for a new group. Their response surprised her. The leader learned she wasn't alone. Other small groups similar in size to hers existed, and this encouraged her.

Meeting together helps leaders gauge how they are doing. Talking about where they are can help them measure their success while allowing them to receive important encouragement from other leaders. Sometimes it is just the lift they need to keep forging ahead.

Providing the Tools They Need

Michael* teaches a small group for couples. Presently they are studying Genesis. The group does not use study guides but relies on Michael's biblical expertise for teaching. Michael tells his members a week in advance which chapter to study. In recent months Michael's busy work schedule caused him to miss some of his group's meetings. He asked Tim,* one of his group members, to fill in for him.

Michael gives the study information to Tim a week in advance and provides suggestions for how to lead the study. He checks back to see how Tim is doing. Michael has come to rely on Tim, who has proven he is both capable and dependable. The two have talked about Tim taking over leadership of the group, which will allow Michael the opportunity to focus on teaching other classes (his first passion) at church.

When a pastor asked Jeff and his wife, Liz, to teach a marriage small group, both knew the church desperately needed it. They saw many couples struggling to hold their marriages together. Though Jeff and Liz were seasoned Christians and church leaders who had led small groups before, neither had experience teaching a marriage study or leading support groups for marriages.

Several of the church's lay counseling ministers worked in a mentoring capacity with the couple to select a marriage enrichment curriculum on DVD. After establishing their group, their meetings consisted of watching a lesson followed by discussion. Jeff and Liz reviewed the week's lesson ahead of time. The coaching they received and the DVDs they used (which came with a leader manual) made leading their first marriage small group easy and enjoyable.

Not only were they coached as they learned to lead their group, but they also became mentors for group members. They frequently drew on their own marriage experience to illustrate healthy marital relationship principles, while clarifying the lesson and answering questions for participants.

Susan participated in a women's small group for over a year since becoming a Christian. She felt called to be a small-group leader though she had no previous experience other than her participation in the group. Susan was not sure how to begin. Since her church had already participated in *The 40 Days of Purpose* curriculum (see resource list in the appendix), which focused on the five purposes of church ministry—evangelism, fellowship, worship, service, and discipleship—the church leadership encouraged the congregation to read *The Purpose-Driven Life* (see resource list in the appendix). The book tied in with the theme of knowing and fulfilling one's purpose as a Christ follower.

---

*Not their real names.

Susan's small-group pastor suggested that she base her small group on studying the book. He provided her with a leader resource that broke the book into lessons and provided suggestions for leading discussions. He periodically checked with Susan, offering suggestions and support.

We talked about the importance of knowing the background and spiritual maturity of a small-group leader before putting the leader in charge of a small group. This is also something to consider when mentoring, particularly when someone is a new Christian.

Tim Burns is an experienced discipler and mentor of new Christians. He has worked with several parachurch organizations in an evangelizing, discipling, and mentoring capacity. He presently ministers at Trinity Church in Lansing, Michigan. Burns says discipling new Christians means considering such matters as, "Do they have a church background? Was it legalistic, apathetic, or involved socially but not grounded in the truth of God's Word?"

Burns continues, "The perspective the person carries with [him or her] will affect [his or her] ability to grasp the truth of the Word. A discipler should take the time to get to know the frame of reference the person carries with [him or her] to effectively communicate."[2] Though Burns's comments refer to training Christians in general to become spiritually mature, much of what he says is also true when it comes to mentoring small-group leaders.

Experienced leaders need less screening and coaching than inexperienced ones, but it's still smart to offer resources, advice, and encouragement, no matter how seasoned a leader is. Staying in touch with developing leaders keeps them motivated and encouraged and is an important part of the mentoring and coaching process. Below are some suggestions for developing successful small-group leaders.

Preparing: Gluing It All Together

No matter how charismatic, how well-liked, or how gifted a teacher, if a leader doesn't prepare, it usually shows in the study he or she leads. Leaders who consider themselves "old pros" are sometimes tempted to coast due to hectic schedules. Soon they're skimping on studying. Ample preparation insures a healthy study. Stress the importance of preparation with both seasoned and novice leaders. Remind even veteran leaders about the value of time spent on preparation.

Research and study tools. A leader's study tools might include a Bible, study materials such as the book the group is using, biblical reference and research guides, a notebook, a highlighter, and paper clips. Online research tools are also invaluable. Biblegateway.com provides multiple Bible translations and is particularly handy for memory-impaired types like me who remember a portion of scripture or a key word but cannot recall where it is in the Bible.

You need only plug in the key words or Scripture portion, choose your translation, and hit the search button and it pulls up many different possible scripture choices. If you are fortunate to remember the passage reference, you can enter that and view several different versions of the same verse.

My husband, Jeff, majored in biblical languages in seminary. He knows how to research the meaning of words in their original language and enjoys teaching studies that delve deep. He's led a variety of basic Bible equipping courses to help people learn how to dig deeper into God's Word.

One of Jeff's goals is to equip people to use these techniques for their own personal study and for leading deeper small-group study. His students love the class format, which allows them to reflect on passages, and they often ask how to study their Bible to get the full illumination of what the author intended.

Expecting group members and leaders to take courses in biblical exegesis isn't realistic, but there are some alternate methods for doing this. In addition to Biblegateway.com, Jeff recommends that students visit Blueletterbible.org. The online resource is more scholarly than Biblegateway.com, which is pretty straightforward when it comes to looking up Scripture passages. Blueletter-bible.org includes a key consisting of buttons with different letters that serve a variety of purposes. The program includes a tutorial explaining how to use this button key. Users can look at a variety of English translations (sorry, no NIV) plus the Latin vulgate. Other options include a dictionary, audio, and an image option for maps and engravings.

In addition to these online sources, older respected study aids such as *Halley's Bible Handbook* and *Strong's Exhaustive Concordance* are available. If you are fortunate enough to have a good church library, you might recommend the librarian add these to the shelves if they aren't already available.

Prayerful preparation. Praying during preparation time allows God to speak through the text so that leaders get a clear understanding of the lesson's focal points and meaning. Leaders should work through their first lesson before the first group meeting. Leaders should prepare far enough in advance to deal with any hitches that might arise—such as their busy work schedules or lessons that take longer to prepare than anticipated. They shouldn't, however, prepare so far in advance that they've forgotten the materials by the time the group meets.

A few days' advance study is ideal since it allows time to make changes while materials are still fresh in a leader's mind. As they read the materials, leaders might highlight or paper-clip (one of my favorite methods) words, passages, or terms that need defining or explanation for their own use or for the group's. They can also note passages that speak to them and that group members may enjoy discussing.

One study method is to read the lesson before writing down any notes and then to go over materials again and make notes. Looking up scripture and cross-references also provides a good lesson foundation. If there isn't time to study the entire lesson in one sitting, break it into segments, studying portions. Leaders should complete the study before the next group meeting.

Encouraging group participation. Encourage leaders to allow group member participation during the lesson. Below is a negative example of lecture format and shows why member participation is important.

A small group took turns teaching their study. One member volunteered to lead the next study lesson at his house. Members arrived in his living room that evening to find an easel with a flip chart. With a pointer in hand, the leader announced, "Please hold all of your questions until the end. I'm going to do most of the talking because I believe the way we have been studying isn't scriptural. Tonight we're going to study the Bible (the implication was that the group hadn't been before he took over). You can ask questions afterward."

Group members sat in stunned silence as the leader launched into his "study," spouting scripture verse after scripture verse that he had memorized. He diagramed his points, making great use of the pointer. He failed to notice the range of stone-faced to storm cloud expressions of pent-up emotions on group member faces as they tried to absorb his "lesson."

Aside from the glaring problem of the "I'm right and everyone else is wrong" format of this lecture, another problem exists. Members frequently have questions as the lesson unfolds. Asking people to hold their questions until the lesson's completion creates frustration. If a teacher continues to teach while one or more students are hung up on understanding the topic, then the lesson's point may be lost completely. How can a student follow the course of the dialogue if he or she cannot get past the first few points?

It's best if leaders address questions as they arise. Sometimes this requires a tight focus to keep the discussion on track. Experienced leaders know that once the floodgates for discussion open, they might have trouble completing the lesson. Perhaps this was one reason the leader in our example asked the group to hold their questions.

Group member participation is important. Few people can learn in a lecture format, especially when the presentation is dry. However, some leaders struggle with groups bubbling over with questions. I suggest they allow for some questions and curb the conversation with a comment such as, "I wish we had time to discuss this further, but we need to move on to the next point."

This way other group members won't become exasperated at the group for constantly following rabbit trails or never finishing the lesson.

The time factor. Managing discussion can be challenging. One of a leader's responsibilities is to guide the lesson and move it forward. The more group members there are, the more aware leaders must be of time during the topic discussion. Discussing an entire chapter in-depth with a group may not be possible because of time limitations. Leaders may only have time to hit on the main points or points that captivate their members' interest. Encouraging members to study ahead of time so they can focus on discussing highlights of the chapter can help.

Developing Shepherds

Group members naturally look to group leaders as role models. Christ called himself the Good Shepherd. Though we've become accustomed to hearing this term as another nickname for Christ's goodness, Christ meant to compare himself to a *good* shepherd as opposed to a bad one (see John 10:11-18). Unlike the hired hand who abandons the sheep at the first sign of trouble, a truly competent shepherd cares about the sheep and their welfare and will take careful measure to make sure they remain safe. Small-group leaders are, in essence, shepherds, and shepherding has several aspects. Good shepherds (small-group leaders) are

Good listeners. Sometimes shepherding requires refraining from giving input and opinions and instead listening to needs and concerns of members. James 1:19-20 says to "be quick to listen, slow to speak and slow to become angry, for man's anger does not bring about the righteous life that God desires." Quiet leaders are often naturally good listeners. Those who are not may need to work on becoming active listeners.

Leaders may have sage advice to give, but if they are always talking, they may miss the important information members may want to share. Good leaders encourage sharing and listen attentively, responding to group members so that members feel they matter and are truly cared for. Comments such as "Oh, I'm sorry you feel that way" or "I've never thought of it that way" can reassure group members that they are valued.

Intercessors. Just as the good shepherd keeps a watchful eye out for potential harm to the sheep, small-group leaders can pray for their group members, their protection, and their spiritual and physical well-being (1 Thess. 5:25).

Burden sharers. Leaders are a source of support and encouragement to group members. They come alongside group members and assist them by providing wisdom and resources to help them overcome and press on toward the goal (Gal. 6:2).

Aware of their own need to recharge. The shepherding role can zap a leader's energy. Every person handles stress differently, and some individuals can perform the same task repeatedly without needing a break. The length of time someone can do this comfortably depends on how he or she is wired. Leaders who know themselves well enough to recognize when they are in danger of burning out usually know when to pull back.

When mentoring leaders, encourage them to look for warning signs that they may need to take a break. Indicators might include a lack of interest in the members' welfare, a failure to prepare lessons, a general callousness toward issues that arise with group members and their needs. In the worst cases it can manifest as depression. These and others indicators may signal a need to pull out for a while. Even Jesus had times when He needed to remove himself from the crowd to recharge (see Luke 5:16).

Making time for reflection and retreat is important. Give leaders permission to occasionally take a break from teaching. A sabbatical might be as simple as asking another group member to teach the lesson for a few weeks, or it might mean taking a longer break of six months to a year.

Lisa Beamer, an experienced small-group leader, observes,

> I think it is so very important that leaders be fed too. Not that they aren't getting something out of the studies they lead, but leading can become a drain on a person if they do it long enough and either don't get a break or don't get the spiritual encouragement they need along the way. For this reason, I've found it necessary to take breaks from leading small groups. I need time to reenergize in order to remain enthusiastic and effective.[3]

Some churches provide leader retreats that allow leaders to physically escape the daily treadmill and spend time in reflection and spiritual renewal. One church I know of holds a retreat every fall at a picturesque lodge set among beautiful aspen and pine woods in Colorado. The retreat starts late Friday afternoon and concludes Saturday evening.

During one such retreat a leader held morning devotions on a leadership-related topic. He chose to look at the life of Joseph as an example of overcoming adversity. At the conclusion of the lesson he asked leaders to choose one key attribute of each leader present. They talked about those attributes and their strong points.

For instance, one leader had a strong gift of mercy, and those present shared examples of how they had seen the leader use this gift to care for others. Leaders talked about how their fellow leaders' strengths affected and influenced them. This affirmation not only helped each person discover his or her own strengths but also gave examples of areas of possible growth.

With today's busy lifestyles, the only way many of us can remove ourselves from the hustle and bustle is if we put a planned event on our calendar. Retreats provide opportunities for pulling off life's hectic path—something many of us cannot do on our own. When forced to rest, we can reflect and spiritually recharge.

Mentoring Pauls and Timothys

I picked up an idea about mentoring and coaching through a writers' network. Applying a concept developed by Dr. Howard Hendricks of Dallas Theological Seminary, this network pairs less experienced writers with experienced ones. Just as the apostle Paul, a mature Christian, mentored Timothy, a less experienced Christian, experienced writers pair up with novice writers to help them improve and grow in their craft.

Paul-Timothy mentoring can work with any type of leader mentoring and can easily be adapted to small-group leader mentoring. To mentor in this way leaders need to complete a short questionnaire. You'll find one at the end of this chapter. Mentoring should be optional. Those who wish to participate match up with partners. Participants can be a Paul mentor (a more experienced group leader), a Timothy mentee (a less experienced group leader), or both (someone who mentors and who is mentored).

The key to the success of such a program is to pair people up with someone who closely matches them but is a step above or below their level of experience. Participants touch base either by phone, e-mail, or in person once or twice a month. Initial contact between mentors and mentees should include a discussion of areas mentees wish help with and suggestions from mentors regarding potential action plans. By working together group leaders can learn leadership skills from each other and build a network of support.

Gathering Your Leaders Together

A church held a small-group leader luncheon for its small-group leaders. The meeting served several purposes: to touch base with leaders to see how they planned to start the new season with their small groups, to see if they needed help with curriculum, and to troubleshoot and swap ideas. As leaders shared about their particular groups, it became evident that the gathering met many needs at once.

You might consider having quarterly or yearly leader luncheons for your group leaders. After eating, those in attendance can spend an hour sharing what is and is not working in their groups. Keep the atmosphere relaxed, encouraging members to give suggestions. The following exercise used by a church served two purposes. It helped group leaders get to know each other while encouraging them to brainstorm leadership challenges.

Scratch and itch exercise. Leaders often have itches (leadership challenges) that need scratching. Following their leadership luncheon meal, leaders were given a small blank envelope, paper, and pencil. They were asked to write down one problem area in their group. This itch represented an area they couldn't reach that they needed relief from. Leaders were asked to place their itches inside the envelope, and then they were told to make an identifying mark on the envelope.

Helpers gathered the envelopes and then redistributed them. People broke into groups. Each group member read from the sheet in their envelope and asked to solicit suggestions from group members as to how to scratch the itch being presented by giving suggestions to the problem. The person reading the problem jotted down these suggestions.

Timed sessions moved the focus to different questions covering all the itches. Then the workshop facilitator called on one person from each group to share their problem and some of the solutions. At the end of the session, someone gathered the envelopes again. The facilitator encouraged group leaders to pick up their envelopes before leaving. Identifying marks made on the envelopes at the beginning of the session by the leaders help them know which ones were theirs.

A scratch and itch exercise is one way small-group leaders can share ideas. The organized program isn't as important as the networking. Your main focus is to provide a gathering where leaders have a chance to swap ideas.

Mentoring and Coaching Basics

Now that we've talked about the more formal ways of coaching and networking leaders, let's talk a little about the informal ways. Those who find the Paul-Timothy mentoring approach too structured and formal can facilitate mentoring and coaching in a less structured manner.

Matching experienced leaders with less experienced ones is the most natural way to pair up leaders. Veterans can serve as a big brother or sister. Introducing one to the other and encouraging them to exchange phone numbers should questions arise is one way to do this. Pulling an experienced leader aside and asking him or her to check in occasionally with a new leader is another possibility. Leader mentors should

Model godly character. Christian principles are more often caught than taught. How a mentor behaves will have a positive or negative impact on a pupil.

"Nothing so completely baffles one who is full of trick and duplicity himself, than straightforward and simple integrity in another," wrote Charles Caleb Colton.[4] We may talk all we want about what makes a good leader, but if behavior doesn't match up with speech, then a leader might do better to keep his or her mouth closed.

Dwight L. Moody once said, "Character is what you are in the dark."[5] In other words, it's human nature to want to appear godly when we are aware that someone is watching, but the way we act when we think no one is watching tells much more about us and our spirituality.

A leader who steps into a mentoring role should exhibit spiritual maturity that exemplifies integrity and dependability.

Be available. Availability includes setting up a time to meet with inexperienced leaders to cover the basics listed above. Coaches can also check in with their partners to see their progress, give encouragement, and suggest improvements. Mentors should listen to any problems mentees wrestle with and make suggestions for working through them.

Touch base. Mentors can informally check up on leaders by asking some of the mentee's small-group members how things are going. They'll no doubt give invaluable feedback. For mentors in larger churches this may involve getting in touch with the appointed person who keeps track of groups and their members.

Listening to what is working and what needs improvement will give the mentor direction about where the less experienced leader may need help.

Leaders Among Leaders:
The Importance of Group Leader Coaches

As you gain more groups, having an appointed contact person and facilitator over all of your small groups can help maintain order and enable good communication and networking. This person stays in touch with leaders and acts as a troubleshooter and cheerleader. Depending on the church's size and its financial resources, this can either be a volunteer or paid position.

As small groups continue to multiply, it will become more and more difficult for one person to oversee all groups. Appointing someone to oversee specific groups can help. Ideally women should oversee women, men should oversee men, couples should oversee couples and perhaps miscellaneous affinity groups.

This position differs from that of mentor. Where a mentor works one-on-one with one group leader, a group leader coach oversees several small groups.

Trisha* is a small-group leader coach. When a need arises in a small group that other small groups might help with, she helps spread the word through e-mail and phone calls. These needs sometimes include serious illnesses or crises among small-group members, resource needs, and so on. Trisha also helps organize and schedule her church's small-group promo table and helps promote small groups. She acts as a liaison with staff to help train small-group leaders and provide resources for the group.

A leader coach can also help schedule, organize, and run small-group training sessions or work in partnership with staff to manage them. When churches have many groups, they may need to appoint a certain number of group leader coaches over a specific number of groups. For instance, you might assign a group leader coach to any of the following: affinity groups, men's groups, couple's groups, and so on. Organizational responsibility will change and morph according to the number of your groups. As we will see, e-mail and mailing list servers provide one final way for networking and staying in touch with small-group activities.

Keeping Group Leaders Connected

What happens between small-group leader networking sessions when there are no meetings scheduled? How do these leaders stay in touch? How do they share needs? One way is for the small-group leader coach to stay in touch with them via phone or personal contact, but this can add a lot of extra work for an already busy coach. Volunteers have limited time to give.

Some churches have online small-group support lists managed by mailing list servers. They use the lists to announce needs that crop up within the small groups, to ask for recommendations of resources for teaching, and to share outreach and missions opportunities that small groups or individual members may wish to participate in. Church members can also share prayer requests through this network system.

These are opt-in lists, meaning group members can sign up to become a list subscriber. The lists also allow them to subscribe and unsubscribe at will. They can choose how they receive their e-mails—through individual e-mail, in digest form with a compilation of the day's postings, or by setting the option for "no mail." The no-mail option allows subscribers to check their mail at the online address for the mailing list server.

Lists such as these need a list moderator. This position doesn't involve a lot of work but puts someone in a gatekeeper position that screens subscriptions.

---

*Not her real name.

The moderator also oversees the list to enforce the rules and remind members to be on their best behavior. They might also have the final say regarding approving members.

You can also use the network to meet general needs of the body. A church might have multiple support lists for different groups, such as one for small groups, one for prayer requests, and one for general ministry needs.

Some of the best mailing list servers to use include

- Yahoogroups.com. Yahoo Groups is one of the most well-known mailing list servers. You can sign up for a list at <groups.yahoo.com>. It's free but not bug-proof, and you must wade through ads when visiting the Web site. Occasionally members complain about delayed posts or that spam filters have filtered out their legitimate e-mails.

- Groups.msn.com. MSN Groups is similar to Yahoo Groups. It also offers the option of creating bulletin boards for specific topics of interest, as well as the general mailing list server, plus a chat feature. MSN's service is also free. MSN is less intuitive than Yahoo Groups and a bit more difficult to navigate, though the multiple bulletin boards are nice for organizing interests.

- Coollist.com works in a similar manner as Yahoo Groups but has fewer bells and whistles. List moderators can view the list of members and add and delete members at will. Their service is free but you must put up with advertising that appears near the bottom of your posts.

- Constantcontact.com is less like a mailing list server and more like an e-mail campaign. It has some great features. Constantcontact.com is a great option if you want to publish an online, subscriber-based newsletter for your small group. The service offers electronic magazine templates and other templates in both text and html format for sending out notices to group members.

   It also has a campaign scheduling feature where you can schedule announcements ahead of time. The service is free for a small number of subscribers and charges a fee according to your subscriber base once you exceed their maximum free membership requirements. You can also inquire about a nonprofit discount.

As you can see, there are many different methods available for coaching and mentoring small-group leaders. Sometimes how you choose to network isn't as important as providing opportunities to network. Having occasional gatherings where small-group members can share may serve the need, even without a planned agenda. Most important is providing the connections and resources. The rest may take care of itself.

Points to Ponder
Small-Group Leader Questionnaire

Below you'll find a small-group leader questionnaire to help determine the needs of your small-group leaders. This questionnaire gauges leader performance prior to meeting with leaders as a group. Use their answers to help plan your small-group leader gatherings so that you effectively meet their concerns and needs.

Name _____

Phone _____ E-mail _____

1. What are your biggest challenges or needs as a small-group leader?
   - ☐ Finding teaching materials
   - ☐ Having others with whom I can share duties
   - ☐ Running orderly and productive meetings
   - ☐ Training apprentices to teach
   - ☐ Planting new groups from my group
   - ☐ Needing a mentor or coach
   - ☐ Other: Explain _____

   _____

   _____

2. We may offer leadership training for small groups. Each session would include a directed discussion about a leadership issue/practice beneficial to all and a moderated open forum to share ideas. Please circle the letter in front of the type of training you would most likely attend:
   a. Quarterly Leadership Luncheons right after the last Sunday worship service where leaders and potential leaders can gather, eat, and share.
   b. A one-day or half-day seminar that covers small-group leadership principles and ideas and includes a meal.
   c. Your choice—which days and times of the week work best for you?
   Days of the week _____
   Times _____
   Frequency _____

3. We need small-group leader coaches to help mentor and coach small groups. Ideally, we would like to have a guy for the men's groups, a woman for the women's groups, and either a male, female, or couple to coach couples' groups and affinity groups. If you would like to help with coaching, please check below.
   - ☐ Yes   ☐ Maybe, if you could tell me more

4. Would you like to start a small group? If so, what would the group's focus be? What resources/people would you need to start one?

Paul/Timothy Mentoring Questionnaire

Please complete the following questionnaire if you would like to be mentored as a small-group leader or if you are interested in mentoring a small-group leader. Mentoring involves sharing ideas and resources about small-group leadership plus spiritual advising and coaching.

Name _____

E-mail _____

Address _____

_____

Home Phone _____

Cell Phone _____

Work Phone _____

Days you are available to mentor/be mentored _____

_____ (mornings/evenings)

☐ I would like a mentor

☐ I would like to mentor

Tell us a little about how and when you became a follower of Christ _____

_____

_____

How long have you been a small-group leader? _____

What groups have you led? _____

_____

part 3
birth, death, and survival

8 birthing and burying groups

Whatever else you do, you must have a
small fellowship to walk with you and fight
with you and bandage your wounds.
—John Eldredge[1]

We saw earlier how small groups resemble miniature churches. Many of the early churches in the apostle Paul's day began through small groups that met in homes.

Church planters typically start with a core group of people that often meets in homes. Launching a church involves hard work. Church planters often begin their work by knocking on doors or making phone calls to connect with those who may want to attend. The church planter works to find a core group of people willing to meet together.

Sometimes church planters labor for years and still only see minimal results when trying to build their nucleus. Much behind-the-scenes preparation and hard work goes into the church-launching process.

Initiating small groups runs a close parallel to starting churches but on a much smaller scale. Both begin with a core of interested people. Leaders must promote their cause enough to propel people to attend their first meeting. From there, hopefully they become regular participants. Despite the hard work, results may still disappoint. Some groups spark and ignite, launching successfully, while others struggle, never managing to bring people to the launch pad.

Houston, We Have a Problem: Failure to Launch

Brandon and Sharon,* a young married couple, wanted to start a small group for other young married couples in their church. They assumed that

---

*Not their real names.

since no group for young married couples at their church existed and plenty of young married couples attended weekend services, there should be enough interest to start a group.

But instead of an easy start-up, they found it difficult to draw people. Their first attempt at gaining members was through a social gathering—lunch at the senior pastor's home. Several weeks before the scheduled launch, they created a bulletin insert promoting the event. Despite careful planning and promotion, no one responded.

But they didn't give up and tried a different approach. This time they planned an outing to a pro baseball game. Surely, this would draw prospects. Again, the announcement ran for several weeks in the church bulletin, and staff promoted the event from the pulpit during the Community Life section of the church service. Despite all the hype, only two couples showed interest in the event. What was wrong?

No doubt they felt discouraged after so much preparation and planning. Was a small group for young married couples a bad idea? Was the timing wrong? Had the church been small, with only a few young married couples, the difficulty would have made more sense. But the church had a weekly attendance of around 500.

Timing is crucial. What could Brandon and Sharon have done differently to get a better response? They might have looked at the timing of the event. Were they trying to launch the group during the summer months when people vacationed? Some couples may have been out of town when the social events took place.

What about the days they had chosen for their social gatherings? Couples may have found it difficult to attend events scheduled on weeknights. The time of day for which the event was scheduled may also have been a factor. In addition, they might have also considered their area's culture, the length of commutes faced by working couples, and what time most people got home from work.

We live in the Bay area where the high cost of living dictates that nearly every spouse work. Due to heavy traffic, commutes can take anywhere from 45 minutes to two hours. Couples might be able to make an earlier event in a rural area, but in an urban setting like ours they may not get home until 7 or 7:30 P.M. These factors affect their availability to attend social events. Even the day of the week and time of day can impact the turnout for group meetings.

Does the launch event connect with the culture and demographics? Let's look again at Brandon and Sharon's small-group launch efforts. Not everyone likes sports. Baseball appeals more to men than to women. Often the woman recognizes a need for marriage enrichment before the husband. Since the woman will most likely be the one who brings the husband to a marriage group, might it have been wise for Brandon and Sharon to plan a special event that appealed more to women?

Would holding the event at the senior pastor's house deter some? Possibly. Since young married couples often have tight finances, it might have been reasonable to ask if young couples could afford to attend a baseball game.

Can you see how important it is to match events with people while considering their interests and financial resources?

Personal invitations work best. I helped our church's administrator catch up with some data entry. Believe me, I don't normally do this and it is not my forte, but Pam nearly drowned in projects and our volunteer staff had dwindled.

I helped out by entering new contact information gathered from the information forms collected on Sunday morning. One of the questions the visitor form asks is how people found out about our church. They indicate whether someone came because of a personal invitation, a yellow page ad, the church Web site, or some other reason. As I keyed in the information, one thing became evident. Nearly everyone who completed a form indicated they had come because of a personal invitation.

People usually get involved in most church-related opportunities—classes, volunteer work, small groups, and so on—because someone personally asks them. We spend vast amounts of energy and time on fancy announcements and printed copy, but in reality, people get involved most often because of personal invitations. I have found this is true with recruiting volunteers as well as with inviting people to events and groups.

Plenty of promo. I have heard that it takes about 10 times the amount of promotion we think something needs to get a new idea across. We may believe we have made a clear promotion when we still hold the big picture in our heads. Promoting and launching events and new groups often requires multiple attempts and methods.

Give at least a month's advance warning to let people know about the group. Tell them in verbal and printed form. Convey a clear explanation of the group's purpose, when it meets, and who people can contact with questions. People often want to know what the group will study. Stating this up front may draw them in more quickly.

Brandon and Sharon might have benefited from more promotion and advance notice in order to motivate people to respond. People are so busy they rarely remember announcements or advertisements the first time. They may not even think to read them! I can't tell you how often I hear people at our own church say, "Oh, I get so busy. I forget to read my bulletin." One can never overpromote events. Well-informed people forget or misunderstand less frequently.

The Battle of the Bulge: Putting Oversized Groups on a Diet

The initial challenge of small-group ministry is launching groups and running them efficiently. Once word gets out about a particular group, people become excited about joining it. Members tell other prospective members about their group—a true example of how personal invitation works best. Eventually though, this personal promotion may cause groups to swell in size (if only more groups had this problem).

A few chapters ago I talked about the ideal group size (of 5 to 12 people). Exceeding this size changes group dynamics. Remember the group I led that grew beyond the comfortable group size? We solved the problem by multiplying and creating a spin-off group. Here's a little more information on how the group grew and the challenges we faced before multiplying.

Our small group experienced significant growth in just a few months. The group met every other Thursday night in different group members' homes. Those who hosted usually taught the lesson. The alternating week format appealed to people with hectic schedules who did not have time to commit to weekly meetings.

As more people joined the group, the atmosphere changed. Some quieter members who had previously shared comfortably clammed up. The larger size also meant less time for discussion because there were so many more people. The lesson took longer because it took more time for everyone to settle in.

Sometimes there was not enough room to seat everyone. Those in small homes could no longer host because of space limitations. The group used to hold social events, some of which included group members and their families. Holding special events after the growth spurt was nearly impossible, since only one group member had a large enough home.

The larger group size challenged us. Though members weren't all that needy, when issues did arise, shepherding members took more time because there were so many more people to shepherd. As a group leader, I realized we could not continue as we had because of space limitations. If we wanted the group to remain healthy, we had to change.

I considered several options. I could close the group and not allow any new members. Or I could leave our membership open and split the group into two groups.

The capping off option. Capping off groups presents some new problems.

First of all, closing off a group does not address overcrowding issues. It just stops future growth. In addition, closed groups can become cliques. You may be familiar with the types of self-focused groups that exhibit the "bunker" mentality.

Members feel safe and comfortable in their foxhole and they don't want that feeling to change. Long-established churches also wrestle with this mind-set. The leadership focus moves from programs and processes that bring people into a relationship with Christ to maintaining existing programs that cater to the interests and comfort of the members.

One has to ask, "Is our comfort and nurture really what Christ has in mind for us, or are we supposed to stretch ourselves out of our comfort zones?"

How about a narrower focus? A leader facilitated a group for those dealing with the loss of a loved one. After several inquiries from prospective new members, she decided to limit her group's membership to only those who had lost spouses. By doing so, members were able to more easily share and relate because of similar experiences. She believed a smaller group size best for maximum effectiveness, so she planned to close the group once they reached 8 to 10 members. One of her group's central needs was to share deep, intimate hurts. She knew her group would achieve this most effectively by remaining small.

The previous example shows there are times when it is beneficial to try for a smaller group size. In most cases, however, growth is desirable and we should take steps to make certain it happens as smoothly as possible.

Earmark future leaders. One way to prepare for growth is to teach group leaders to watch for potential leaders within their group; then groom those prospects for leadership. Should the time come to start a spin-off group, the process will be more streamlined because of these ready-made leaders.

New groups gel easier when leaders come from within the group rather than from outside. Leaders who formerly participated in these groups already have immediate rapport with their group members and understand the group dynamics. Leaders of groups that are ready to multiply might consider the following tips to facilitate the multiplication process:

Expect resistance. Members in healthy groups bond and view other group members as part of their family. The mere mention of splitting often causes members to panic. When one leader announced to group members that she planned to multiply the group, a worried group member wrote her an e-mail arguing against it. Here are some of the concerns this person raised.

If we split now, do we have enough people for two groups? We just got new people to join our group and it seems as soon as they started, we are splitting. I'm not sure how good this is for these people who don't yet feel a part of the group. I realize we are a group of leaders, but we also need to be fed . . .

. . . My original reason for getting involved in this group was so that I could learn. I keep hearing that we should grow and branch off to keep the growth and I agree, but I also want to make sure that we aren't all branching off just to lead our own group . . .

. . . I want a group that I can feel secure in as a family . . . I felt this was working just fine and don't think that the growth of each individual will be hindered by adding a few families . . .

This group member had a negative experience with a previous group spin-off. He mentioned this in his letter and referenced a drop in attendance. He observed, *"I never got the family feeling back again."*

Many members join small groups for support. They fear change that threatens their "family" closeness. Their complaints may seem like a tempest in a teapot to seasoned leaders; however, these members feel their concerns are valid. Never brush aside their worries. Prepare in advance to address these concerns and manage them with diplomacy. By doing so, you will defuse their fears and ease the way to multiplication.

Prepare the soil. Preparing members for the initial split means less resistance in the end. Begin preparing members for the break by talking about how much the group has grown. Mention what experts see as the ideal size—5 to 12 members—and how group dynamics change when groups exceed this number.

Finally, talk about some of the new challenges the group size presents, such as less time for sharing, space challenges, and people feeling less comfortable sharing. You can mention all of these concerns in months preceding the multiplication.

Set a group size limit or goal. Discuss concerns of the growing size of the group and what, as a leader, you feel is the breaking point. Use anticipatory, forward-looking speech: "If we get one more couple . . . ," "If we get two more people . . . ," "We will probably need to start another group," or "We really need to think about starting a new group."

Use positive language. Talk about it as positively as possible. Avoid terms like *split* or *divide,* and use terms like *multiply* and *spin off.* I joked with our group members that we wanted to create a spin-off group such as in a successful television show and later teased members that they had spawned a new group.

Pray. Blanket the group in prayer and enlist others to pray. Pray over group unity and peace for the decision. Ask God to pinpoint who should lead the new group and that this leader would step up to the position if asked. Pray with group members during the meeting on the day the break takes place.

Coach. Once you select your new group leader, talk with him or her about the responsibilities. Put it in as positive a light as possible, but be honest. If the position is more facilitative than leadership-oriented, then say so, but don't gloss over duties. Explain what the leadership involves and offer to mentor and coach the new leader to help him or her step in. Potential new leaders will listen more receptively to taking a leadership position if you can make it seem as easy and seamless as possible.

Just as you prepared your group, you want to prepare your leader. Hand off any materials such as the group roster of new members, suggested group guidelines, values, lesson materials, and so on.

Make the break. One of the hardest parts of small-group multiplication is knowing how to divide the group. Do you do it by age of group members, their children's ages, where they live, or randomly? Do you let members choose which group they belong to?

After a lot of thought and prayer regarding our group's growth issues, I decided that drawing names was the best way to create the spin-off. I based my decision on biblical examples. Joshua cast lots when helping distribute the land of Canaan to the tribes of Israel (see Josh. 18:10). You'll find other references to casting lots in Prov. 16:33 and Acts 1:26.

We placed the names of all group members in a bag, with the exception of the existing group leader and the leader of the new group, and then we drew names. I assured members that if they were not comfortable with their newly assigned group, they could move over to the group of their choice. (No one did.) Looking back, it appears as if God's divine hand chose which group members went to which group. He knew in advance the issues some of these group members would face and which leaders and groups would be able to best meet those needs.

Ease separation anxiety. To ease the separation anxiety of dividing up their small-group family, our new groups decided they would still have occasional social gatherings. This helped sooth some of the more worried group members. The groups planned to meet every other week on Thursday nights as we had done previously. But they wanted to operate on a staggered schedule so that on one Thursday night one group would meet while on another Thursday night their sister group would meet.

They would also continue to study the same book. Group members were given the option of dropping into each other's groups if they had a conflict and could not make their own. Members liked this idea because it meant they would still interact with each other even if they were assigned to different groups.

Members most concerned over the group's multiplication seemed relieved to know they would still interface with both groups, so they were at peace with the decision.

One final tip for making the transition go smoothly—leaders should not give group members too much say in whether or not the group will multiply. When it comes to change, most people would rather not. Christians habitually overlay their culture onto biblical operations. In America this surfaces as a belief that when making decisions, even those pertaining to church, we should handle them democratically. You won't find this method in Scripture. Biblical leaders often made decisions they felt were best for the group.

Churches that allow members to have a say in every matter of business frequently find themselves embroiled in divisive disputes, often over trivial matters. With this in mind, allow small-group members to express their concerns and have a say, without creating an environment where the situation is ripe for dissent and conflict. Sometimes it's best to make an executive decision without group input, but it should always be done after prayer and reflection.

Letting Groups Die

Nature has seasons of birth, maturity, and death—from the verdant green of spring where everything bursts with life and energy to the dying process of fall, when life becomes subdued. If spring represents birth, then winter symbolizes death—with its gray skies and dormant and seemingly lifeless trees.

Just as nature has its life cycles, so do churches and ministries, and small-group ministries are no exception. A few years ago my husband and I served a small church with a declining population in Pennsylvania. Even in its most vibrant days the church population scarcely topped 150 in attendance. When we arrived, the church was declining in membership. Once filled with families of young children and teens, the population had grown up, graduated, and moved away. Even some of the longtime older members had moved away due to retirement. Most of the remaining members were over 50.

When the church originally purchased its property, founding members believed the surrounding woodlands would eventually develop into housing complexes. The neighboring property, however, was eventually rezoned for commercial use. Office buildings and strip malls stood where church leaders had envisioned neighborhoods. In a last attempt to make changes and keep the church afloat, the leadership brought in an expert to evaluate where the church was in the church life cycle. What I learned during the evaluation process changed how I viewed church ministry and my own views of effective ministry.

I now know that churches go through a natural process of birth, growth, maturity, and decline, comparable to spring, summer, winter, and fall. In the early years everything is new and fresh. Churches may struggle to stay afloat, but those that do eventually get to a point of steady or rapid growth. This summer season is one of the healthiest, and growth can also cause some struggles for leaders as they try to create order and manage operations. Nevertheless, no matter how vital a church has been, it will eventually reach a point where it levels off and then declines.

We've already looked at launching small groups. You might call this the spring season of small-group ministry. Groups that reach a stage of growth and maturity where group numbers swell and may indicate a need to multiply are in the summer phase of small-group ministry.

In general church ministry, as churches head toward fall and winter, leaders, especially those who remember the days of exciting growth and change, may feel discouraged, even blaming themselves for the decline. But time passes, area demographics change, neighborhoods change, and interests change. Members grow older and so do their children. Ministries that once met the needs of the people may no longer meet their felt needs.

To keep church ministry relevant and effective, leaders must stay informed about activities both inside and outside the church walls. This includes keeping tabs on a church's demographics and culture and the felt needs of the people. Continuing to do ministry the way it has always been done guarantees the preservation of an assortment of sacred cows that no longer address the needs of the congregation or its surrounding community.

The more aware leaders are of these cultural and demographic matters, the greater the chance they will be able to jump the downward curve, reverse the decline, and bring the church back to thriving health. Jumping the curve is difficult, especially for a church on the lower side of the downhill slope of the church life cycle.

Reversal is still possible, but it is usually easier for a church to close its doors and for new churches to be started.

These same principles apply to small-group ministry. Here is just one example.

A small-group leader who managed a men's group had facilitated the same group for almost eight years. During its peak years the group was a great equipping and fellowship resource for Christian men, especially fathers. The group helped them develop a godly lifestyle and taught members how to apply Christian principles to work and home.

Over time group membership dwindled. The leader had more and more difficulty getting men to attend the scheduled group meetings. What changed? Did the leader lose his passion for leading? Did people's lifestyles get busier? Did he fail to adapt his teaching style to the fathers' changing needs? It's difficult to say. Any or none of these things may have caused the decline.

After trying several promotions and changes to draw new interest with no improvement in attendance, the leader finally decided it was time to end the group. The group had served its purpose and he needed a sabbatical. The good news is that today this leader is still active, teaching classes and using his leadership skills in other areas of ministry.

We often think that shutting down any ministry is bad and that by doing so we have somehow failed. In truth, birth and death are all part of the ministry life cycle. Ministries cannot go on indefinitely. Sometimes letting a group die is the best thing we can do because resurrection comes out of death and burial. New groups that are more in tune with the current needs of members may launch and free former leaders to minister in other areas.

Churches should continually evaluate the effectiveness of their ministry as a whole and this also includes small-group ministries. Keeping a group alive just to keep it alive serves no good purpose other than to placate those who remember the ministry when it thrived. Take note of which of your ministries are healthy and which are not. Though letting go of ministries that are no longer effective is painful, doing so prevents exhaustion and futility. We should never fall into the habit of trying to find warm bodies to run them—a bane of many established churches. If you have ministries like this, take a serious look at why they are still here. Closing down outdated ministries releases leaders to start new ministries. Your church may benefit.

Points to Ponder
Are You Maintaining a Sacred Cow?

1. If your church presently has small groups, can you identify the seasons they are in? List the groups you know of and the categories you would place them under.

Spring	Summer	Fall	Winter
Just Beginning	*Thriving and Growing*	*Shows Signs of Age*	*Needs to Close*

2. List any sacred cows, that is, ministries or groups that were once vital that you feel may need to close down.

Explain why you think so.

3. In what ways can you help facilitate the launch of new small groups?

9 troubleshooting

Most certainly you will face one or two problems—
perhaps even some serious ones—in leading a small group.
Effective group leaders recognize that problems
they encounter are potential growth points
for the individual as well as the group.
—Dr. Henry Cloud[1]

Small groups have many positive aspects. They provide a life-changing environment and a support system where members can share struggles and encourage each other. Through their nourishment members develop and grow spiritually, and even improve life skills. Small groups also build a sense of family and community.

Despite these many benefits, groups also have negative aspects. Where numerous personalities congregate, the chances of conflict and misunderstanding increase. Even the best small groups wrestle with issues. Some relate to group dynamics. These tears in the group fabric happen for any number of reasons.

Most of the time group members and leaders can navigate around the cause of the problems, but sometimes they may need assistance to work things through. The purpose of this chapter is to help leaders deal with challenges their groups may face from time to time. Suggestions on the next few pages will assist in working through any existing problems and/or learning how to avoid similar problems in the future.

Dwindling Group Membership

One day I absentmindedly tossed a wool sweater into the wash. The sweater came out clean but considerably smaller due to serious shrinkage. The sweater might have fit a small poodle. Small groups sometimes have shrinkage problems, too, as the number of group members dwindle.

After our large group multiplied and birthed a new group, my husband and I took charge of the spin-off group. Prior to breaking for Christmas, we talked about multiplication with the old and new groups combined and worked out how they would divide.

We planned for the old group and new group to start meeting again after the New Year. When the time came for our first meeting, a new couple delighted us by attending. Imagine our embarrassment when none of the other members assigned to this new group showed up. Our first group meeting felt awkward as we studied our lesson with just the two new group members whom we hardly knew. The husband had never before participated in a small group.

During that first session I worried that I had made a mistake in my decision to divide up our larger group. We felt the jarring sense of loss of community and bonding. Because people didn't know each other, there was no family feeling. Discussion didn't flow with so few people to add their thoughts and keep it moving. As a leader I felt as if I were sitting in public in my underwear.

The group actually turned out better than the first meeting indicated it might. I learned later that several group members who would have attended couldn't that evening because of conflicts. And though I had sent an e-mail reminder, one couple forgot. The experience underscored the importance of having a comfortable group size. With so few members in attendance the feeling of family was missing. Before our next meeting, I phoned and reminded absent members that we had missed them and I encouraged them to attend the next meeting. The good news is that our group became well-established and grew to a more comfortable size.

In our group, dwindling membership occurred due to restructuring. In addition, some group members had conflicting commitments right after the holiday season. Phoning members to remind them of what they missed got them back on track. Our little hiccup was just a hiccup and nothing more, but some groups experience small numbers regularly.

Shrinking group membership happens for numerous reasons. Perhaps a group never attracted enough members to begin with, or a group lost members over time. People may have moved away or had time conflicts or found that the group didn't suit their felt needs. Numerically challenged groups can cause members to feel uncomfortable and strain how well they relate and function together. When groups have fewer members, even faithful members may eventually want to drop out. Meetings become dull and predictable. Gone are the lively discussions that hold people's interest and the sense of camaraderie.

Without knowing exactly why a group's membership is shrinking, it is hard to fix. Some churches develop small-group coaches or facilitators to work with the leaders of small groups to mentor and encourage them. Others have small-group networkers visit small groups and sit in on meetings. Doing so gives them a feel for what is working well and illuminates issues groups may need help with. I'm not a huge advocate of networkers because of our church's experience.

When our church tried enlisting representatives to visit groups, members seemed guarded and uncomfortable. It was like having a school principal sit in on a class. Less intrusive ways to check up on a group may involve handing out questionnaires to group members to get a feel for how things are going. You can use the questionnaire at the end of this chapter for this purpose. If a group has shrinkage problems, this questionnaire might help determine the cause. Below are more factors that can also contribute to group shrinkage.

Poor teaching. Sometimes groups shrink in size because of poor teaching. Lack of preparation, poor lesson organization, or teaching in a lecture format that excludes members from participation can contribute to membership decline. If members don't speak up to tell the group leader why they are dissatisfied, people will continue to drop out.

Both small-group coaches and group members can make suggestions for teaching improvement, but they should do so with sensitivity and diplomacy. If they see specific areas where a group leader can improve teaching skills, they might gently point those out to the leader.

Churches are in the business of equipping leaders, and one way to train new leaders is to help existing leaders improve their teaching and leadership skills. Group members learn by observing. If their group leader does an excellent job, they will learn teaching and leadership skills simply by participating in their group.

Poor curriculum. Sometimes despite a leader's best efforts at screening materials, they just aren't what the leader expected. If enough members complain about materials, the leader may want to listen to what they say. I had this happen with a women's Bible study I chose on women in the Bible. The writer seemed to skim over many of the deeper issues some of the characters faced. Some of my group members pointed this out, and I had felt this as well. We resolved the problem by continuing to use the book while also talking about and examining some of the meatier issues the scripture passages raised.

The leader can either try to add his or her own insights to improve the materials or opt to choose something else.

Prolonged studies. My husband participated in a men's group that studied the same book for over two years! The group had chosen a devotional study with a golf theme. Group members kept taking study breaks to participate in golf outings. Outings can add zest to a group, but too many interruptions can also drag out a study. Numerous or lengthy interruptions, such as summer breaks or holiday hiatuses, can drag out the material. Members may get bored and drop out—which is precisely what happened with several members in the golf group.

Group leaders occasionally make the mistake of selecting a study that covers too much material. Many groups promote their new studies in the fall after school starts when people return from vacation. If a group is already partway into its curriculum, it is difficult for someone new to join without feeling out of sync.

In addition, group members who have participated in the study may grow tired of the topic if it stretches beyond a year. A solution to lengthy material is to either skip chapters or cover two at each meeting. One exception to stretching a study beyond a year is if group members are enjoying the study so much that they beg to keep going.

Group members can't make the meetings. A drop in attendance is normal. People start out with good intentions but stop attending due to conflicts. Some group members may be too busy to attend weekly small-group meetings. Or the meetings might occur on a bad day for them.

If attendance decreases, the leader might ask members (and those who drop out) if holding group meetings on a different day would work better. One shouldn't shift meetings just for one person, but if several have issues, it might be worth making a change. Moving meetings to every other week and another day might be the answer.

Group members are bored with the study material. Leaders should carefully select lesson material for several reasons. A study should capture group interest, meet felt needs, and be simple enough for members to grasp, but it should also be complex enough to challenge group members so they don't become bored.

Group members are intimidated by the material or teacher. Margaret,* a small-group leader's wife, confided she was disappointed that their group had dwindled in size. I remembered her husband, Jim,* from a class Jeff and I taught at church. Jim's IQ was off the scale and made me feel as if I had the mental capacity of a pebble.

He was a biblical scholar who loved to delve deep into theological issues and debate about them. His approach and questions often emphasized knowledge for its own sake over the practical applications to which most people could relate. Sometimes by the conclusion of our class, Jeff's and my eyes were glazed over from trying to deal with Jim's intellectual banter.

Several young Christians had joined Jim and Margaret's group. I suspected Jim's love of intellectual study and his teaching style and interests failed to mesh with his group members' mental capabilities, interests, and needs. Mem-

---

*Not their real names.

bers who couldn't handle feeling intellectually lost and disconnected during his lessons chose the easiest solution. They stopped coming.

Sometimes the material is the problem. Sometimes the teacher is the problem. Sometimes the problem lies in a combination of the two. Matching the academic level of the material with the intellectual and educational level and interest of members is crucial. Jim's students probably felt overwhelmed and intimidated by his inability to teach on a level they understood. He might have succeeded had he been teaching kindred spirits. By promoting his group as one for intellectuals seeking to think deeply about scriptural principles and to research them thoroughly, Jim might have drawn the right match for his gifts and styles and more successfully connected with his students. But it was not a match for young Christians.

Reduced group membership is not the only challenge group leaders face. Because of the diversity of personalities in a group, leaders often must cope with the quirks that come with them.

Those Challenging EGR Members

Pastor Rick Warren refers to troublesome or needy people within the Christian community as Extra Grace Required people (EGRs). EGRs are those who, for one reason or another, always seem to require extra patience, grace, and attention. Some EGRs are downright dysfunctional and hard to love, while others simply have irritating idiosyncrasies for which we must make allowances. Nearly every small group has at least one EGR member. Warren jokingly says that if you can't identify who the EGR person is within your own small group, then it's probably you![2]

The more new Christian converts your church has, the more EGRs you'll have. On a good day, quirks of EGRs who participate in small groups can make meetings run over their allotted time because they dominate and/or monopolize time group leaders intended to spend on something else. On a bad day EGR members can be so needy and demanding that the remaining members never want to return to the group.

Consider some of the following examples taken from real-life encounters with EGRs.

The case of John and Sue.* John and Sue were members of a couples' small group. Within a span of a few months, John and Sue lost their home in a flood and John went on disability for a back injury acquired on the job. Doctors diagnosed Sue with chronic Fatigue Syndrome. Their misfortunes contin-

---

*Not their real names.

ued as Sue broke her leg and spent the next year in a cast because it wouldn't heal. John and Sue also had to place their youngest daughter in a facility for emotionally disturbed children. John got a job, lost it, gained another, and lost that one in a matter of months.

Chaos and bad choices perpetuated their misfortune. During group prayer time their need for sympathy sucked remaining group members dry. Members did their best to bear the couple's burdens, but they grew increasingly heavy. To paraphrase Spock from the movie *Star Trek II: The Wrath of Khan,* "The needs of the few in the group outweighed the needs of the many." Even when they shared during Bible study time, John and Sue managed to turn the attention to their issues.

The case of Anne and Sandy.* Anne and Sandy loved to talk. Both were storytellers who shared prayer requests about many people they knew who needed prayer. Their colorful commentaries included unnecessary details about the people. Their requests often took so much time that other group members had to cut their prayer requests short or could not share them at all.

The case of Angie.* Angie, a devout Christian, knew Scripture well but was also very self-righteous and judgmental. She loved teaching scriptural principles, but her teaching method consisted of spouting scripture and lecturing. Group members felt condemned and ostracized if they disagreed with her. After she joined their group, no one wanted to share for fear she would berate them for not being holy enough.

These are just three examples of EGRs. You may also know a few. The technique for managing EGRs depends on the person, group, and problem. Here are a few general suggestions:

Address the EGR. Don't ignore EGRs. Unattended EGR problems can suck the life out of groups. Work through the problem right away so it doesn't grow into a larger one.

Remind group members about the rules. Group members may forget the group's guidelines and rules. Periodically remind them of the group's purpose and operational guidelines. (What? No guidelines? Maybe it's time the group wrote some.) Doing so may not resolve big problems, but it may assist with smaller logistical issues such as not starting or finishing on time or not respecting the needs of other members.

Pull the troublesome group member aside. Talk to the EGR member privately about the disruptive behavior. Be kind but specific. Explain why it is a problem and suggest changes in behavior the member could make.

---

*Not their real names.

Talk with the remaining group members. Proverbs 15:22 says, "Plans fail for lack of counsel, but with many advisers they succeed." If an EGR continues being disruptive after you have spoken privately with the person, take the next step. Often by this stage one or more group members may have already brought the concern to your attention because they find the behavior troubling as well.

An option for you would be to talk with other group members and explain that the EGR's self-focus dominates and disrupts the group. I'm not suggesting you hold a private meeting without the EGR present. If the EGR learns of it, he or she may feel that people are scheming against him or her. But you can talk with group members individually, encouraging them to help (quietly) steer future meetings, wresting the attention away from the EGR and minimizing the chances for any one member to monopolize.

For instance, if the needy group member hijacks group meetings by asking for too much prayer time for themselves or by going off on tangents during study time, encourage members to keep the conversation on track so that the problem member has less sway. You, the leader, are the shepherd. Shepherds sometimes need the help of sheep dogs to get people to work together and head in the same general direction. Appoint some reliable group members to help herd these wayward sheep.

Set boundaries. After you talk with the EGR member and group members separately, talk to all members at the next scheduled group meeting with the EGR present. Explain to members about having consideration for other members, urging them to limit their requests and length of sharing time during prayer. Soften this request without finger-pointing by talking about your concern regarding the group's tendency to get off track during lesson time.

At this time, you can also publicly ask all members to help steer the discussion to stay on topic. Even though this has already been done privately with all group participants except the EGR, doing so again restates the rules and makes everyone accountable so that the meeting stays on track.

Use banning as a last resort. People who visit online chat rooms are expected to behave. If they act inappropriately, a moderator bans them from future postings—at least for a time. If they have too many infringements, they may be permanently banned. The same rules should apply to small-group participation. If, after talking with EGR group members and giving them several chances, they fail to change their troublesome behavior, you may have no other choice than to ask them not to attend your group anymore. Use this solution *only* as a last option.

A group shepherd's first concern is for the welfare of all the sheep. If the need of the one outweighs the needs of the many, something is out of balance.

Another group may suit this person's needs better. If the EGR needs help on a much deeper level than a small group can provide, you can make recommendations for more professional help.

Galatians 6:2 encourages us to carry each other's burdens. Bearing one another's burdens and stepping over into codependency where you help perpetuate the problem is separated by a narrow margin. By continually giving needy members more attention, we feed their need and shortchange other members. We also send a message that the needy person comes first. The dysfunction and demands of one group member can seriously strain the health of the group. As a group leader you must weigh the needs of all members along with the needs of the EGRs and do what is best for the majority.

Before concluding this section, let me offer a word of caution. By talking with EGRs about the need to modify some of their inappropriate behavior, you may offend the EGRs, who may then choose to leave the group. Pastoring isn't always easy and includes these types of risks. You should never intentionally cause someone to leave the group, but if he or she does, it may actually be a blessing in disguise. Just as pastors must look out for the welfare of their church members as a whole, small-group leaders must do what is best for the group. You should feel no guilt if the other responds by leaving.

Leaders may also wrestle with handling group discussions full of conflict potential. Here are some thoughts.

Managing Lively Discussions

"Boy, did our small group ever have a lively discussion at our last meeting," Debbie said. She and her husband, Dave, are seasoned church leaders. They had just started a small group several months earlier.

"What did you discuss?" I asked.

"We've been studying 1 Corinthians and we have one couple in our group who is pretty young in the Lord. When we got to the part about homosexuality [see 1 Cor. 6:9], Dave said that God views it as an abomination."

"He used those words?" I made a face. Dave was most likely recalling a related scripture passage from Lev. 18:22. (The King James Version uses the term *abomination* in regard to a man lying with a man.)

"Unfortunately he did and it raised the hackles on one guy in particular. The discussion got pretty, uh, lively."

"You mean heated?" I asked.

"No. I think it stopped just short of heated." Debbie was not sure how their next meeting would go. I thought for a moment and then said, "Maybe Dave should not have used the term *abomination*. Although I know God believes homosexuality is wrong, Dave's word choice probably came across as self-righteous and possibly condescending."

We talked for a while. Both of us agreed that society believes homosexuality is acceptable. Many people today are not as schooled in the Bible as people once were. They view those who see homosexuality as a sin as narrow-minded and judgmental because that's what society believes.

"Remember the story of the rich young man?" I reminded her. "He asked what he needed to do to be saved and Jesus told him to go and sell all he had and follow Him. The young man went away sad because he didn't want to give up everything he owned. He found Jesus' words hard to swallow.

"The same was true of many of Jesus' followers. When Jesus told them He was the Bread of Life and that the only way to eternal life was by partaking of that living bread, many left. To this, the disciples exclaimed, 'This is a hard teaching. Who can accept it?'" (John 6:60). I supported Debbie and Dave's stand and told them so. I talked about the importance of explaining to group members that homosexuality is a sin. But I urged them to convey that it is the sin and not the sinner that God hates. The *abomination* label applies to many sins to which believers are susceptible, not just homosexuality. No sin hierarchy exists.

A disturbing revisionist trend is taking shape today where some Christians edit out unpopular or unpalatable beliefs or issues on which the Bible takes a stand. God's Word says that we must enter through the narrow gate, not by a large highway (Matt. 7:13-14) and that Jesus Christ is the only way in through the gate (John 14:6). Sometimes taking a stand and sticking to what the Scriptures tell us makes even believers go away saying, "This is a hard teaching."

Some who wrestle with these tough biblical truths may choose either to find another church or to opt out of following Christ completely. We are tempted to say, "Well that's OK then. If you find that hard to swallow, just ignore it." Society would tell us that those beliefs today are intolerant. How should small-group leaders handle this? They should

- Choose words carefully when people disagree with what Scripture says. If possible, avoid words that inflame and spur on heated debate.
- Exhibit self-awareness of their own susceptibility to sin. Avoid finger-pointing. Remember that Jesus cautioned us to remove the board from our own eye first. For example, a small-group facilitator might point the finger back at himself or herself and say, "This is what I believe about this passage."
- Stand firm. Following Christ has never been popular, but it is important. Leaders may have to take some flack.
- Give the debater more scripture to research the matter. For instance,

Debbie and Dave might have suggested the group member look at some additional scriptures that dealt with homosexuality and then said, "You'll need to come to your own conclusions."

Another possible solution to managing lively discussions is for leaders to ask staff members or those with the spiritual gift of teaching to attend one of the group's meetings and help facilitate during a tough questions time. Sometimes those who have more biblical knowledge and training can field tough questions better than the average layperson (and with a bit more diplomacy). An authority may lend credibility to the discussion and help individuals work their way through issues they may wrestle with.

Occasionally lively discussions occur when group members disagree on the biblical interpretation of a passage. Some passages have clear meanings, while others do not. Handle discussion carefully to avoid divisions among group members or creating wounds that will not heal. If the discussion gets too heated, group facilitators should halt the discussion and pray with members, and then move on to another passage or topic. The facilitator can offer to meet separately with the individual(s) in question. Or they can make a statement that the group members probably won't reach a consensus, and that is fine. Sometimes we must agree to disagree to preserve unity.

Differing Stages of Spiritual Growth: From Milk Suckers to Carnivores

Leaders must use wisdom and diplomacy when managing EGR members. The two also go hand-in-hand when determining how to manage the different spirituality levels of group members.

Groups with members on the same level of spiritual maturity are rare. Some people are at the milk stage of Christian maturity, while others are ready for meat. How can group leaders address the needs of people at different stages of discipleship?

Leaders must decide how deep they want their group to go, remaining sensitive to members' spiritual journeys without caving in to demands of specific members. If a leader chooses to keep the study at a basic level and some group members feel it's not deep enough for them, the leader might recommend a different group for those who want to go deeper. If deeper spiritual study confounds a less mature Christian while most other members are comfortable, the same rule applies. The less experienced Christian may feel more at home in another group.

Another solution is to study deeper and at a slower pace, remembering to explain concepts in as simplistic a manner as possible. Or a leader may assign a more mature Christian to disciple the newer Christian provided both the potential disciple and potential coach agree to the idea.

The group leader might also ask members to indicate when concepts become too deep so that he or she can more clearly explain them. No two Christians grow at the same rate. Some brand-new believers soak up Scripture and theology and grow at warp speed. Others who have been Christians for a long period of time remain spiritual infants because they do not wish to study the Word or spend time on deeper concepts.

Familiarizing yourself with where each member stands will help you disciple them in the best way possible.

Changing Channels: Managing Leader Burnout

We've looked at important factors that strongly affect how well a group functions: dwindling group membership, EGR members, and even the battle of the bulge where groups strain at the seams. Our troubleshooting chapter would not be complete without exploring one more concern that affects the health of small groups—leader burnout.

Leaders are similar to athletes. They train and exercise to get into shape and may even eat a special diet to become fit. Like athletes, leaders need nourishment and equipping. Despite their training, even the best athletes can become weary, and overwork increases risk of serious injury. They may need to rest in order to go to the next round of competition.

Leaders also need to take breaks. How much and how often depends on the leader's personality and makeup for the length of the marathon he runs.

Some leaders, like long-distance runners, are capable of doing the same thing over and over without tiring. Others are more like sprinters. They do well for the short term, but leading a group for the long haul may exhaust them. Keep tabs on your leaders' progress.

Indicators of burnout. Every leader experiences discouragement at some point, and this is a normal part of leadership. Leaders might feel disappointed if group members fail to meet expectations, attendance lags, members fail to study, or if they don't show any signs of growth. Lingering discouragement often signifies a deeper problem—leader burnout.

Indicators of leader burnout include grumbling, poor lesson preparation, canceling group meetings, or impatience with group members. Fatigue and frustration are also signs. A leader may be reluctant to admit these feelings or share them with others in leadership because he or she fears they will react negatively. "What do you mean, you're getting tired of leading? If you don't do it, who will?"

Though no one voices these opinions out loud, they are often quietly implied. Sure we need leaders, but shaming someone into continuing to serve is only going to build resentment on their part.

Give leaders permission to take a break. Work with them to find a replacement, either a temporary one—someone who can stand in for a few lessons—or someone who can take on more long-term responsibility. If no replacement is possible, the group might merge with another group (if they are compatible and willing) or you might give the leader permission to close the group.

Giving former leaders new purpose. Leaders burn out on occasion because they no longer feel challenged by what they are doing. Don't force anyone to stay in a leadership role. When a leader steps out of a leadership position, he or she often finds another place to lead. Leading is often a part of leaders' makeup, and they remain champions for small groups even if they feel called to use their leadership skills in another capacity. Here are some examples of small-group leaders who went on to new roles.

Art led a small group for years and loved doing it, but he began to feel a stronger tug toward one-on-one discipleship and teaching. When he shared this with his pastor, they decided to move him toward ministry where he felt a stronger calling. He first equipped a group member to take over group facilitation. Then Art sat in on his church's spiritual gifts classes to train to become a spiritual gifts instructor.

Once he felt comfortable, Art began to teach the classes. Art also wanted to implement leadership training and felt that one of the best places to start was by working with small-group leaders. He and his pastor worked together to develop short lessons focusing on leadership and maturity values, and Art presented them at small-group leader meetings.

Julie* taught a women's small group for nearly 11 years. As can be expected after such a lengthy tenure, she began to feel more drained than energized by teaching. She worked with her pastor to identify and equip several coleaders of the group so she could step out of the leadership role. Today the group is still going strong.

Julie never stopped leading. She simply stepped into another position, which still involves small groups. She helps plan her church's small-group networking and training sessions and checks in with groups to troubleshoot and report any concerns to her pastor. Her service has helped her busy pastor stay in touch and oversee the groups and their leaders.

We've looked at potential problem areas that occur. Every small group has its own identity because it is made up of so many unique individuals. When

---

*Not her real name.

people commit to follow Christ, we frequently expect immediate transformation, forgetting that maturing is a process. Small groups are like families, and every family member has lovable traits plus annoying quirks. The brokenness experienced in the lives of members before they became Christ followers trails into the small-group family setting.

Expect dysfunction, but don't allow it to make your group dysfunctional. Having led small groups myself, I have experienced the frustrations that come with trying to maintain healthy groups. Sometimes it's easy. Sometimes it's incredibly draining. For the sake of leader health and group member health, stay engaged in caring for the welfare of small-group leaders and the welfare of their group members.

Points to Ponder
Troubleshooting

For small-group leaders. Choose one problem mentioned above or another problem you have seen small groups wrestle with and write it down below.

1. What suggestions do you have to help resolve the problem?

2. What would you do if you needed help troubleshooting a problem with a small group?

3. Is there someone who could give you advice? If so, who?

For small-group members. On the following page is an example of a small-group list that leaders can use to query small-group members regarding room for improvement.

How Are We Doing?
Small-Group Evaluation Form

Here are some questions to help your church leadership get a reading on how well their small groups are doing. Please have group members *and* leaders fill the questionnaire out and turn it in to the group leader. The group leader should also make copies and give them to his or her small-group coach or supervisor.

Group Info

1. Group Name _____

2. Our group has _____ members.

3. This size seems: ☐ a bit large; ☐ a bit small; ☐ just about right.

Lesson

1. Our leader has the lesson prepared: ☐ always; ☐ most of the time; ☐ rarely.

2. Our study material is: ☐ almost always interesting; ☐ somewhat interesting; ☐ not very interesting.

3. Our study material is: ☐ excellent; ☐ good; ☐ fair.

   Explain: _____

   _____

   _____

4. Our group and/or leader: ☐ uses a variety of teaching techniques and methods; ☐ could use more variety or different methods when teaching.

5. Suggestions for how your leader can improve the lesson: _____

   _____

6. Are you willing to help teach a lesson? ☐ Yes; ☐ No; ☐ Maybe

7. What do like about your small group? (You can list several things.) _____

   _____

   _____

8. What suggestions do you have for improving the group, including how it functions as a whole? _____

   _____

   _____

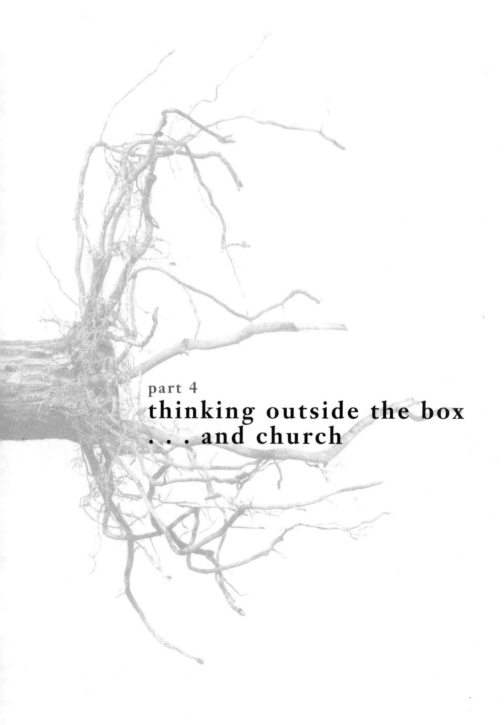

part 4
thinking outside the box
. . . and church

10   out of the holy huddles and into the world

Christianity has been practiced in the midst of our "holy huddles." There is a lack of Christian energy being expended on reaching the lost. We are using it all up at our gatherings.

—Bob Muni[1]

The small town we reside in has a typical small-town feeling of warmth and security. Sometimes it is entertaining and sometimes it is annoying because everyone knows everyone else's business. Despite the small-town atmosphere, our town is unique because it's nestled in the populated San Francisco Bay area.

We have only to drive five minutes to experience tons of traffic, shopping malls, and commercial and entertainment distractions. Many of our town's inhabitants delight in the way things are. They want to preserve the current way of life, desiring neither more development nor more growth.

Land in the Bay area is particularly precious and expensive. Without regulations and laws to protect the open space, housing developments and commercial construction might quickly swallow up the remaining undeveloped land. Instead of taking ambling walks over golden hillsides, we'd be driving through a sea of cookie-cutter houses—not an appealing prospect.

Because of this, the public meets any mention of new development with outcry and a movement to block it. Local residents have adopted a "hunkering down in the bunker" mentality, wanting things to remain the same. Our church fought a long battle to build a real church building (as opposed to renting a warehouse) on nearby pastureland. We are on this new property, but it took an enormous amount of time and financial resources because of the bunker mind-set of those opposing the change.

Frequent moves have left my husband and me geographically far away from extended family. In our early years of marriage I found this very painful. But as the years have passed I have come to realize that the small groups we have belonged to have been a wonderful family support network. In many ways we have become closer to the people in our small groups than to our own family members because of their availability and compassion. Still, this closeness also has a downside.

Just as our small town wants to preserve its small-town feel of comfort and security, once we start feeling comfortable with our small groups and those bonds begin to strengthen, we are tempted to sit back and bask in the secure feelings they give.

A leader at a small-group leader networking session spoke about his group's need to multiply because of their numerical growth. His wife and several other members opposed the multiplication. They didn't want the group to lose its intimacy and warmth.

People need an environment where they can feel cared for and safe. The danger is that when they become too comfortable, their primary concern becomes their own welfare and how to keep that feel-good atmosphere. When their main focus is their own well-being, it's hard to care about others.

Long-established churches often suffer from this malady. After years of having vital ministry, churches may morph into a social club where people's main concern is feeling comfortable. Though some members may still have a heart for reaching unchurched people, they often don't know how to go about it because they are so entrenched in old habits and systems.

Leaders can prevent this from happening in small groups by training members to see beyond themselves and consider the welfare of others.

Stepping Outside the Circle of Comfort

Congregational members may already be familiar with the Great Commission, which states, "Therefore go and make disciples of all nations, baptizing them in the name of the Father and of the Son and of the Holy Spirit, and teaching them to obey everything I have commanded you. And surely I am with you always, to the very end of the age" (Matt. 28:19-20). But even if they know it by heart, we need to remind them that reaching out to others is a part of every Christian's responsibility.

Some argue that a small group is not the right place for evangelistic focus. Evangelism may not be the primary concern of small groups, but it can still encourage members to reach out, since all Christians are urged to share the Good News.

What better place to teach people to put feet on their faith? We often fail to reach out because we don't know how. Small-group members' diverse gifts and skills can actually help them share ideas and enthusiasm for caring for others.

People with the gift of mercy have a heart for people's welfare. Compared to their compassion, the rest of us may feel callous and indifferent.

Those with the gift of evangelism reach out to share the Good News with relative ease, while many of us struggle with how to go about it. Because many uniquely gifted people participate in small groups, varied gifts and passions abound. Some may have the heart and know-how for reaching out through compassionate ministry or missions-related ministry. Small-group leaders can note those members who naturally gravitate toward these interests; then harness their enthusiasm and compassion. They can use these people to organize and champion special outreach and compassion types of activities so that remaining group members participate.

Members not endowed with these unique gifts often feel stretched, but that's not necessarily a bad thing. When people come together for a common cause, it's amazing to see what can be done in Christ's name. Holding special care and compassion events are one way of getting people out of their holy huddles. One of the most basic ways, however, to reach out to others and prevent the bunker mentality starts with something very basic—the room-for-one-more attitude.

Room for One More

Later chapters talk more about the challenges of open groups, but I believe that briefly focusing on them here is important. Keeping an open membership (continually allowing more people to join a given small group) rather than capping it off at a certain number is one of the first safeguards to preventing holy huddles. It helps teach members to care about the welfare of others.

When new people join a group, existing group members must automatically readjust their thinking to include one more. Doing so prepares them for future outreach. When members bend their wills to allow one more, they are more likely to develop hearts concerned with reaching others for the Kingdom.

The "World" May Have Infiltrated Your Group

A group leader decided that during his group's first meeting he would have every member tell the story of how he or she became a Christ follower. Imagine his surprise when several members explained that they were still seekers and hadn't made that decision yet. Amazingly, one of the members who made this statement died of a heart attack only a few days later. Fortunately, during the group meeting, that member had heard several people tell their faith stories.

No one knew if this man made any kind of commitment to Christ after hearing his group members' faith stories, but it was reassuring to know he had the opportunity to think one more time about what it meant to follow Jesus. Just because a group is church-related doesn't mean group members have made a commitment to follow Christ. Sometimes instead of us going out into the world, the world comes to us. Leaders should not automatically assume that all group members are already Christ followers.

Small groups can be a discipling environment not only where people grow in maturity but also where non-Christ followers make a decision to commit their lives to Christ. Group members who alert leaders to the spiritual standing of prospective members can assist those leaders in knowing how to talk to those members during meetings.

Leaders who know their members' spiritual status in advance can avoid Christianese (the Christian language and concepts so alien to many unbelievers and new members) and heavy biblical concepts, and explain what these concepts mean as new members assimilate into the group. With a little care and a lot of prayer, these members may eventually make a commitment to Christ.

A new couple wanted to join a small group. One of the group members told the leaders she felt the wife was a Christian but wasn't sure if the husband was. This immediately alerted the leader to look for clues for where the prospective new members stood spiritually. After the new couple joined the group, the leaders were sensitive to teaching scriptural principles they might otherwise have assumed the husband already knew, while tuning into where he was spiritually.

I'm not suggesting that leaders ask members if they are Christians before allowing them to join their group. That would put potential new members on the defensive. Nor is excluding non-Christians the solution. To learn where members stand, a leader might have each member tell how he or she came to Christ in the first group meeting. Like the leader who did this in a previous example, group facilitators may learn that not everyone has made that commitment. Another way is for leaders to talk with other people who may know the new members. They may be able to give valuable spiritual background info.

We may not think of a small group as an evangelism field, but sometimes it can be, and it's best to be prepared and aware of where members are in their relationship to Christ.

Outstanding Outreach Opportunities

The world doesn't always come to our door, although, in the previous example you can see that it sometimes does. If we want to reach out to others, we must usually go out into the world.

The church I grew up in occasionally held evangelistic drives. Leaders of these scheduled campaigns expected church members to go door-to-door presenting the gospel. I hated participating in these events, but to be counted as a good Christian I joined in the efforts. I was very shy, and this was way outside my comfort zone. I don't remember anyone ever coming to Christ through the campaigns. Why? Because they did not establish relationships with people.

Many Christians still think of door-to-door canvassing when we talk about evangelism and outreach. Maybe this is because the Great Commission tells us to go out and make disciples and our idea of going out is traipsing from house to house. When we meet someone for the first time, however, it's difficult to build rapport in one meeting so that the person wants to hear anything we have to say about the gospel.

Evangelism isn't necessarily a door-to-door event. Why would God ask us to do something so unnatural for us and at which most of us perform poorly? Evangelism and missions go hand in hand with benevolence (caring). They are often so parallel in their interests that it's hard to tell where one ends and the other begins.

Evangelism's main purpose is to reach non-Christ followers with the Christian message. Many people think of missions as doing evangelistic work for third world countries; however, many mission opportunities are present in our neighborhoods, churches, and schools. Small groups can experience the joy of reaching out and giving in a variety of ways.

Our church participated in a program called 40 Days of Community (see resource list in the appendix). The campaign's key focus is to build community primarily through small groups by encouraging them to reach out through acts of service in the community. Individual groups decide where and how to do this. While evangelism's central purpose is to tell others about Christ, benevolence work is more concerned with the physical needs of the less fortunate, though people may enter a relationship with Christ because of the compassion individuals or groups show them.

People worrying about where their next meal will come from or needing medical attention have difficulty hearing the message if their needs are overlooked. Jesus said, "For I was hungry and you gave me something to eat, I was thirsty and you gave me something to drink, I was a stranger and you invited me in, I needed clothes and you clothed me, I was sick and you looked after me, I was in prison and you came to visit me" (Matt. 25:35-36).

James 2 talks about the importance of caring for people's physical needs. "What good is it, my brothers, if a man claims to have faith but has no deeds? Can such faith save him? Suppose a brother or sister is without clothes and daily food. If one of you says to him, 'Go, I wish you well; keep warm and well fed,' but does nothing about his physical needs, what good is it? In the same way, faith by itself, if it is not accompanied by action, is dead" (vv. 14-17).

Benevolent outreach allows small-group members to put feet on their faith, take the focus off themselves, and concentrate on the welfare of others. We shouldn't participate in acts of kindness to ease our guilty consciences because we feel we haven't done enough or are trying to earn heavenly brownie points. By reaching out, groups develop the healthy habit of caring for others and touching them with Christ's love.

Benevolence Brainstorming

Hands-on charitable giving and involvement can be much more powerful than writing out a check for charity. This is because the giver sees the transformation firsthand and doesn't hear about it from some other source. Hands-on care and compassion allows those involved to feel they have a part in causing that transformation. People are energized when they participate in person because it moves them from passive giving to active giving.

When our church began 40 Days of Community, some small-group members were skeptical. They grumbled about having to find a community service project. After going through the study and participating in a project, the skeptics had a change of heart. We saw remarkable results. Our small groups took on a variety of projects, everything from serving Thanksgiving dinner to the underprivileged to cleaning up a widow's junky backyard.

We found that when groups set aside their own interests and focused on others, they experienced a joy of giving that spilled over onto the recipients. In many cases the contact changed lives, all because these groups decided to do something selfless.

One group learned about a wheelchair-bound man who needed a ramp built for his mobile home. The man and his wife had just purchased the trailer but could not navigate the stairs, so they could not move in until they had a ramp. The small group got a local lumberyard to donate the lumber, and they built a beautiful ramp. Without the group's help, it is hard to say when the man would have moved in.

In another case a woman at another church managed a "coffee shop" for teens in their church parking lot. The church was on the direct route for many high school kids after school. Volunteers set up tents and offered free coffee and snacks to over 400 kids every Thursday afternoon. The town also had a second high school for at-risk teens who had not faired well in the more traditional high school.

The same woman who managed the parking lot coffee shop wanted to minister to the kids from the second high school too. When she learned what our church was doing, she put the word out to our small groups and asked for help. One group responded.

Now, every Thursday afternoon group members stand inside the high school lobby at dismissal time serving nachos, chatting with kids, and snapping their photos. They created a photo album the kids love to look at and are slowly building relationships with these tough and often troubled teens. The door is opening for talk about spiritual matters. The future looks promising for this ministry.

Have small-group participants share some of their stories with your church members and small-group leaders to fuel excitement about charitable acts. Their accounts will motivate others and make them want to do more. We've seen our members' community involvement skyrocket. They have learned how to move out of their own self-focus and care for others outside the church. Though the 40 Days campaign is over, people still want to serve. Small-group missions and care is still making a difference in the lives of our attendees and the people they touch.

The 40 Days campaign stretched people to think about others outside of their comfortable surroundings. The first hurdle to move people to benevolence and mission-mindedness is to train them to become alert to opportunities and needs. The next step is to teach them what healthy care and compassion involvement looks like.

Perhaps you have heard the expression, "Give a man a fish and you'll feed him for a day. Teach a man to fish and you'll feed him for a lifetime." Sometimes, to clear our consciences, we look for ways we can give back. Simply giving handouts, however, may not be the best kind of help because it can make people more dependent on us and less likely to try to improve their own circumstances.

In many ways the United States welfare system worsened this type of problem. Though welfare started with the best intentions and did indeed serve a good purpose, it helped perpetuate dependency. After all, why would people want to work if they could get food and other necessities for free?

Some charities provide conventional opportunities for people to help through handouts, while others provide opportunities to help people improve themselves. Groups that take on charitable projects should look for organizations that use contributions to actually help people improve their conditions. Results can be so much more effective than simply giving a one-time gift that makes people dependent on more gifts.

Groups might want to establish special guidelines when working with needy individuals. Brokenness comes with the package. Too much neediness can be unhealthy for the givers. Give group members permission to say no and set boundaries if the circumstances call for it. They shouldn't put themselves in a codependent situation where their acts of kindness enable unhealthy habits or circumstances in the recipients. Teach group members to ask themselves, "By doing this kindness for this other person, am I giving them a handout or a hand up?"

Granted, sometimes we must give the handout before we can give a hand up, but making members aware of the pitfalls of care and compassion can also be prudent.

I also caution groups to make sure that the perceived need is real and that the assistance you intend to give is welcomed by the recipient. I know of a group that helped a widow with some home upkeep. The woman had recently lost her husband and she cried most of the time the group was there, humiliated by their assistance. Though she may have truly needed the help around the house, she was not emotionally ready. Group members sensed the awkwardness and learned a valuable lesson.

Make sure your intentions to do group projects don't tread on someone else's feelings. Groups should verify with the other party first that they are open and willing to receive assistance. Here are a few benevolence activities to consider.

Lunches for the homeless. A church in our community schedules a monthly event where their small groups pack and deliver brown-bag lunches to the homeless in the downtown San Francisco area.

Habitat for Humanity. Habitat for Humanity offers one of the best opportunities to help impoverished people gain a leg up. Habitat is a nonprofit, nondenominational Christian housing ministry. The organization's purpose is to eliminate poverty housing and homelessness and to make decent shelter a matter of conscience and action. The organization has built over 170,000 houses around the world and much of it has happened because people volunteered their time and resources to make it possible.

Individuals and groups can schedule workdays with their local Habit organizations to assist with their building projects. Labor involved might include painting, building, or even cleaning up after construction. To find out how your group can get involved, you can check their Web site <Habitat.org> for organizations in your area.

Adopt-a-Family. Many variations of Adopt-a-Family and other similar charitable opportunities exist. We'll start with Adopt-a-Family first. Some churches call this the Angel Tree. Opportunities for this ministry usually arise around the Thanksgiving and Christmas season. Ornaments or tags are placed on a Christmas tree in a church lobby with the names or gift requests for needy family members.

People select an ornament or tag and then purchase requested items, bringing the gifts back to a drop-off area, often the church, where they are later delivered. People can participate as individuals, families, or groups. Groups have sometimes gone above and beyond the requests by securing donations for Christmas trees, sending along cookies or refurbished bicycles, or even offering to help deliver the presents.

No official national organization called Adopt-a-Family exists; however, many churches use this ministry name to designate this type of ministry. If your church doesn't presently have someone organizing such a ministry, small-group members can create their own Adopt-a-Family opportunities by contacting local schools, organizations, and even the police in your community to find out the names and needs of families who might benefit from additional charitable help.

Adopt-a-Child. Where Adopt-a-Family opportunities are usually local and hands-on, other similar organizations that allow you to contribute to the welfare of the underprivileged by "adopting" them (at least in principle) are also in place. You pay a specific amount per month or year. Many of these organizations pair you up with a child and you can often correspond with them as you contribute to their physical welfare or education. World Vision is one such organization. Presently they offer the opportunity to adopt a child for a mere $30.00 a month. Imagine the difference a small group could make in the life of a needy individual or child simply by giving a one-time donation or a few dollars a month. It could be as simple as passing a donation can around during your meetings.

Here are some options for getting involved. You can send a child to school for a year for a mere $50.00. You can buy a share in a drinking well for $100.00. You can buy a rabbit for $15.00. You can purchase an emergency aid kit for $100.00 or buy a basic needs kit for only $15.00. There are many options, and the contribution amounts greatly vary according to the opportunity. To learn more, go to <worldvision.org>.

Send a care package. A small group wanted to show their support and encouragement for troops overseas. One member checked with the local Red Cross to learn about their current needs and where they could drop off packages. Group members who helped organize the care package contributions sent a list of suggested items, provided by the Red Cross, to other group members.

Items on the list included nonperishable snacks, hard candy, warm socks, CDs, books, games, and more. The group learned that many of the countries the packages would go to had strict regulations about no overtly Christian material. Group members who wanted to contribute Christian CDs and books chose those with covers that appeared more secular in hopes that they would pass through screening without any difficulties. Members brought all items to a specified group member's home, who then delivered the care package to the Red Cross drop-off.

Visit a nursing home. A small group skipped their usual Christmas party and held a caroling party at a local nursing home. Before their visit, each group member brought cookies to one member's home where they assembled cookie plates to bring to the residents. Once there, the group performed favorite Christmas carols (even taking requests) and then presented the cookies to residents. To the delight of the residents, group members also brought their children, and following the caroling, and to the delight of the residents, they spent a few extra minutes socializing with the residents who decided to share their cookies.

Help women and children in crisis. A women's small group collects personal hygiene items for a women's shelter. Since battered women and their families often have to leave their homes for safety at a moment's notice, they cannot always bring these things with them. Items the group donates include toothbrushes, toothpaste, soaps, small bottles of shampoo and conditioner, hairbrushes, and other small necessities. In addition, the group learned of a dry cleaner that often had nice, unclaimed clothing. By collecting the coats and suits that might have otherwise been discarded, the group provided professional-looking apparel for women trying to reenter the workforce.

Just as battered women have to leave their homes quickly, children in the foster care system often have to leave a location at short notice with only the clothes their backs. After learning about some of the needs of foster children, I researched a benevolence project for my small group that would help foster children and allow for hands-on participation. I was surprised to learn that there was a nonprofit organization in my town that supported foster children with extras. One of their programs allows you to buy pillows for children, plus stuffed animals that they can have for their own.

I talked personally with the woman in charge to find out their specific needs. In addition to pillows and stuffed animals, I asked about providing backpacks that we could fill with special items.

She loved the idea. They preferred to stuff the backpacks themselves and requested that we bag items or bundle them by category. Small, safe games; a change of clothing; towels and washcloths plus personal hygiene items are appreciated gifts.

Additional needs include birthday gifts, school photos, music equipment and lessons, yearbooks, and more. In addition to the pillow donation program, the organization has a mentoring program where people can befriend older foster children, teach them life skills, and help them research colleges and scholarships.

Though this is a local program, there may be a similar foster child support organization near you.

Car care. This is a perfect activity for a men's group. Hold a car care day and provide services for those who cannot normally afford decent car care. Services offered might include free vehicle inspections, oil changes, chassis lubes, or other minor maintenance. You can schedule events once a month, quarterly, twice a year, or once a year.

Food bank or soup kitchen. Nearly every sizable community has a food bank. They might be managed by a city mission or by a church. Small-group leaders can check the phone book yellow pages or with churches in the community to see if they participate in either a soup kitchen or a food bank. Food banks especially often need help on certain days of the week or month organizing and preparing food for distribution. Soup kitchens are usually open to receiving help with food prep and serving. Like many nonprofits, they get the bulk of their volunteer help around the Christmas season, so they might appreciate help during the off-season when help is in short supply.

Remember your local soup kitchen if you have an event and have large amounts of leftover food. On several occasions I know of groups that brought their surplus spaghetti, salads, and breads to a soup kitchen. The managers appreciated the donation.

Around the holiday season if your church is lucky enough to have its own kitchen and large dining area, several small groups might want to join together to cook a holiday banquet for underprivileged families in the area. Or small-group members can cook meals in their own homes and make arrangements to deliver them to specific families. Groups can even do this in collaboration with Adopt-a-Family donations so that they deliver meals and gifts at the same time.

The same organizations that have food banks often have additional charities they run, such as secondhand stores. Sometimes they may also need help with cleaning, pricing, and sorting donated items. In other cases they may appreciate volunteer cashiers.

Prison ministry. Several members of a small group volunteer at a local prison. On Sunday morning members bring their message of encouragement and hope to inmates. They share Scripture with them and help lead a Bible study. At home, other volunteers help grade study lessons completed by inmates.

We often think of the victims of crime as those who had the crime committed against them, but in many cases the families of the perpetrator suffer as well and are frequently left to deal with the shame, grief, and financial ruin brought on by the bad choices of their loved ones. Family members must often fend for themselves. If incarceration lasts for a lengthy period, the family may face financial crisis.

Small groups can check with the police in their community to see if they know of families who may need extra help. It could be something as simple as providing a coat for a child who needs one or extra money for school supplies.

Yard sales for charity. When spring-cleaning time comes, many people have yard sales. Most of us really don't need those extra stored items hanging around. Joining forces as a group to sell and donate garage sale items is a great way to raise funds for a charitable cause. The group should discuss what they would like to do with the proceeds prior to holding the sale, plus they will probably want to publicize it, stating what part of the proceeds will go to charity and more specifically the charitable organization that will benefit.

Short-term mission trip. Many churches have missions opportunities where groups can go to specific regions for a short time to volunteer and help bring the gospel and physical aid to residents in that area. These short-term trips provide opportunities for small-group involvement, from fund-raising and preparation to going on the trips themselves. I've even heard of entire families participating in short-term mission trips in lieu of their regular vacation. Participating in a short-term mission project can be life-changing. When people see firsthand the humble accommodations in which most people in third world countries live, they return with changed values and a softened heart toward missions. If your church doesn't offer such opportunities, or you would like to learn about additional opportunities, here are some suggestions:

- **Hope4Kids International.** Hope4Kids has traveled to countries such as Romania, Russia, Haiti, and Cuba. Volunteers ranging from teens to retirees compose their mission teams. They have a special need for medical personnel, since part of the ministry involves bringing medical care and medicines to families in these countries. During a trip to Cuba, mission team members donated six computers to a school that had none.

  Students had the opportunity to learn vocational skills that would help them secure better jobs. As is often the case, when people learn about Hope4Kids, they catch the vision and want to help. When one small-group member who umpired baseball in his spare time learned that Cuban children had no baseballs to play the game, he rushed home and gathered up a box full of 45 baseballs for a departing mission team to take with them.

  People love to get involved in helping the less fortunate and are often waiting to be asked. Those who wish to participate in Hope4Kids go through an application process and this includes a $200 processing fee, which is the case for many short-term missions. Once accepted, Hope4Kids gives participants a packet with instructions and ideas for raising all of the funds necessary for a mission. The organization also provides home missions opportunities. For more information, you can visit their Web site at <hope4kidsinternational.org>.

- **U.S. International Ministries Group.** The U.S. International Ministries Group (USIMG) is the missions branch of the Navigators. The Navigators is an apostolic and multicultural organization that focuses on bringing the gospel to all nations. USIMG offers both short-term and long-term missions trips. The short-term trips are called Stepout.

  Short-term trips are a great way for groups or group members to get a taste for missions and make a specialized contribution. Short-term opportunities include missions in the United States, such as their summer camp counseling programs in the inner city or trips abroad to numerous countries such as Norway, Argentina, Africa, and elsewhere. To learn more go to <http://www.usimg.org/> or call (719-594–2447).

- **Adventures in Missions.** Adventures in Missions is an interdenominational short-term missions organization. Their objective is to mobilize and equip the Church for missions by bringing the mission field to the Church's doorstep. The explanation on their Web site states that their short-term missions will "**Expose** [you] to opportunities to **encounter** God and **experience** a passionate relationship with Him; as you're **equipped** to see the world through God's eyes and seek to discover His **mission** for your life; and you're **enlisted** to respond to God's call within the context of your life."

  Adventures in Missions provides adult mission trips for mixed adults, men's groups, women's groups, and family missions to countries such as Ghana, Kenya, Native American reservations, Dominican Republic, Puerto Rico, and more. For more information visit their Web site <adventures.org> or call (1-800-881-2461).

Small-group members form bonds, a healthy part of being one in the Body of Christ. But when group members become too comfortable and self-focused, they may morph into a holy huddle. Sometimes you need to stretch group members and urge them to see beyond themselves and to consider the welfare of others outside their group. When they grasp the concept of agape (unconditional) love, the results are often transformational, both for the members and those they reach. The next page includes questions group leaders can use to help them think about ways their group can reach out to others. Use them to consider possibilities for benevolence, evangelism, and outreach.

Points to Ponder
Moving Away from the Holy Huddles

1. What projects has your small group been involved in over the past one to two years to help them focus on others besides themselves?

2. What are some ways you can get your small-group members to think about benevolence or evangelism opportunities?

3. List four possible ideas for benevolent or outreach opportunities in which your group might be able to participate.

4. Write down the month or months in which you might want to schedule these events.

5. List four steps to making at least one of these events happen:

    (1)

    (2)

    (3)

    (4)

11 unique groups, unique methods

One denominational leader met with 25 rather discouraged churchgoers. He asked them what clubs and organizations they belonged to, and what offices they held. They were amazed to discover how influential they were, as a group, in their local community. Could they use their networks to advance the church's mission?
—Michael Moynagh, *emergingchurch.intro*[1]

Many churches approach small-group ministry from the inside out, establishing small groups from within the church body. Most people who join small groups are already a part of the larger church fellowship. They may connect with a group after a promotional pulpit announcement or printed small-group listing. Or they receive a personal invitation from another church attendee.

People become involved in groups for several reasons. Some want to connect with other people on a more intimate level; others long for deeper teaching. Often they want the support and care found in a small-group community. Still others may attend their first small-group gathering out of curiosity. "Just what is all the hype about small groups?" they may ask. They decide to try a group out and see for themselves.

The preceding pertains to people already part of the church scene, even if their attendance is sporadic. But what about the monumental numbers of people resistant to church who aren't a part of the church community and may never be? Are small groups a possibility for them?

As a small group neared the conclusion of their study course, the leader sought her group's advice about what direction to take. She had led different small groups for the past four years and was thinking about taking a break. Unsure, she decided to talk about it with her group members. "If we do continue to meet together, what would you like to study? Do you have any suggestions?"

Most of her group members were willing to study the topics she suggested. But one woman suggested they hold a study that would allow them to invite neighbors. She wanted to connect with unchurched people. Neighbors seemed like a good place to start.

Emerging Trends and Relationship Building

The woman who wanted to include neighbors in her small group had a heart for reaching unchurched people. What better way to reach non-Christians than to invite them to a small group? Often new Christians have very little biblical training. One would think that foundational studies covering basic Christian beliefs for new Christians would also work for those outside the church. In some cases they might.

When trying to reach the unchurched, however, it is much easier to connect with them if the stigma and barriers caused by the church structure are out of the way. People avoid church for many reasons. Some raised in church might have gotten out of the habit of attending. Some may have been active in church and were hurt because of church dysfunction. Others may have had bad experiences due to strict, regimented church traditions, rituals, and restrictions. Still others, because of having no church upbringing, may never have even considered attending.

People approach religion and spirituality like consumers, picking and choosing what they believe based on personal preference. They frequently borrow bits and pieces of belief systems from the available smorgasbord of spiritual beliefs, creating their own religious foundation.

A generation with no Christian torchbearers cannot pass on Christian heritage and biblical precepts to the next. One generation is all it takes for Christianity to die out. If a young person's parents do not attend church or talk about Christ, that young person may be partially or completely ignorant about Jesus Christ and His teachings. When he or she marries and has a family, there will be no knowledge of Christianity passed on.

Michael Moynagh in his book *emergingchurch.intro* cautions that the traditional "inherited church" is dying. If church is to avoid extinction, we must look at fresh expressions of church—new ways to connect with the people living in a consumerist world. Church leaders can no longer take the "you come to us" attitude. We must adjust our thinking to a "we'll come to you" approach.

At the heart of these new expressions are smaller "churches" that are in many cases nothing more than small groups. Moynagh explores the myriad of ways churches, particularly those in England, are finding ways to connect with people. Many of these new expressions involve small groups that connect with specific cultures. A majority of these groups also place a strong emphasis on missions.[2]

We live in a world saturated in consumerism, and the emerging church seeks to subvert it. A key way to do this is through caring and relationships and making genuine connections.

Reggie McNeal, author of *The Present Future,* recognizes this need for relationships. To paraphrase, McNeal feels that churches shouldn't be program-oriented as much as they are relationship-oriented. Relationships will make a difference. For it is through relationships that we build bridges and genuinely connect with people.[3]

Pastor Rick Warren often says, "People don't care how much you know until they know how much you care."[4] What good is telling people about God's plan for their lives and Christ's sacrifice for them if they have physical needs overshadowing the hollow words we say?

A short-term missions team to Mexico learned this important lesson first-hand. Several people paired up and went door-to-door inviting poor people to a Christian gathering. Two members of the team talked with a man and invited him to an evening service. The man told them he had never attended such a service before. Then he asked them if they had medicine to treat a large infected sore that he had on his arm.

"No. We're sorry. We don't have any medicine," replied the two mission workers. As they walked away, both felt the Holy Spirit urging them to do something for the man.

Upon return to their base camp they told the story to other volunteers. There they learned where the nearest "pharmacy" was. The walk was a long one, and the mission center didn't generally give funds for medicine. The two workers decided to pay for the medicine themselves. That afternoon in the hot Mexican sun, they walked the dusty road to the pharmacy where they purchased medicine for the man. Then they returned to the man's home and treated his wound with an antibiotic salve that they let him keep.

That evening they were surprised when the man showed up at the service. Later that night he made a commitment to follow Christ. If it hadn't been for the two volunteers who felt a strong urging to meet his physical needs, the man would probably never have come.

"People don't care how much you know until you show how much you care." If more of us took the attitude of these two volunteers, whether at home or on the mission field, perhaps more people would see our words as genuine.

People often sense when Christians target them for conversion. We might as well put a huge bull's-eye on them. So often we see them as statistics or a goal we want to achieve. Win one more for Christ. How much more effective we would be if we focused on relationship-building, taking the time to find out about the needs of the people we are trying to reach. We may need to start with physical care and make a long walk to a pharmacy.

Connecting with Their Culture

One of the drawbacks of the inherited church is the expectation that people will adapt to the inherited church's culture. We think people will feel comfortable coming to our unique style of worship service, dressing the way we dress, and behaving the way we behave. When this doesn't happen, we are disappointed.

One executive pastor shared at staff meeting, "I've invited him to church several times, but he never comes." We often make the same mistake, thinking that after meeting someone after one or two times that we can either lead them to Christ or get them to come to our church. Though in some cases this may happen, in reality very few people come to Christ in this fashion.

Only after a relationship-building investment is progress made, and despite the relationships we build, many people still may never make the trip to our church. We may need to take the church to them.

If we build community first, the door may open to the subject of spiritual matters. One place to start this connection process is through a Matthew party. I am not sure who coined this term, but it refers to the type of gathering that Matthew the tax collector held. He invited a mix of his unsaved friends, many tax gatherers like himself, and other believers. He invited Christ too.

We are reluctant to invite unchurched people to our social functions because it takes us outside of our comfort zones. How will they behave? What if they do something really embarrassing, use bad language, get drunk, or reject what we believe? We squirm thinking of the possibilities. But connecting with unchurched people is what Christ did best. He rubbed shoulders with all kinds of people and took great interest in them. Once He built a rapport with them, He then broached the subject of spiritual matters.

Jeff and I attended a Matthew party hosted by a friend named Peter. I'm not sure Peter was even aware that it was a Matthew party. Peter plays drums for one of our worship teams. He had just moved into a new home and threw an open house to celebrate. He invited a mixture of church friends and people he knew from other, nonchurch associations. Peter also plays jazz in a secular ensemble, and he and the two other group members set up their equipment at the open house and provided some musical entertainment.

Before they began to play we had the opportunity to mingle, and we struck up a conversation with one of the guitarists. He was what I call a hip dude. In addition to moonlighting in the band, he worked days for a nonprofit organization that served people with special needs. Having worked for a couple of different agencies that served people with special needs myself, I connected with him about the importance of treating these clients with dignity and learning to value them as individuals. One thing led to another and before long this gentleman talked about spiritual matters.

During our discussion it became apparent that he had some rather odd, new age ideas. The subject of Jesus never arose. Still, he freely talked about this higher power, relating it to human spirituality. Had time permitted, we could have had a really deep conversation and he may have wanted to hear more.

Matthew parties such as Peter's are a good starting point for connecting with people and getting a foothold on relationships. Then those relationships can provide the connections needed for inviting people to other functions, such as small groups with a specific focus. Not everyone invited will come, but some may.

In an earlier chapter we talked about affinity groups and how much more successful they tend to be because of natural interests that people find in common. Secular groups such as these are a great way to establish connections with a specific culture. When I say culture, I am not merely talking about another nationality. Culture can include nationality, education, salary level, lifestyle, and more. Peter's friend was entrenched in the jazz and rock music culture. Music was one of his natural connecting points.

We can learn plenty from Jesus—the Master of connecting with people.

Bringing Bible Basics to the Unchurched

Secular affinity groups can limit how much we share spirituality. Barriers may exist that prevent us from talking about spiritual matters because of the location where we've made the connection. For instance, we may not feel free to talk about Christ in a club or workplace setting because of workplace regulations and/or time constraints. General closed-mindedness of the individual to the topic of Christianity can also stand in the way.

Some have found that the best way to share foundational Christian beliefs is by creating a specific group forum where basic beliefs and biblical questions can be approached.

One of the fastest-growing venues for these types of groups can be found in Alpha Groups. The Alpha Course began in the United Kingdom as a way of reaching unchurched people. With so many opposed to stepping into the traditional church, Christians in leadership had to find a way to present the gospel in a nonthreatening manner. The format used is an effective one and depends on who is hosting the course for how the event unfolds. Typically the leader invites a small group of people to attend a light meal, after which they share a lesson that runs approximately 45 minutes (presented either live or prerecorded on DVD or videocassette). The course usually spans 11 weeks. People come for a variety of reasons: to investigate whether God really does exist, to learn what happens after death, or to even grasp a better understanding of the basics of the Christian faith.

When the course concludes, some groups decide to keep meeting. People may join the larger church body or may go on their way. In some cases people may attend one session and then decide it is not right for them. (See the appendix for more information on the Alpha Course.)

Alpha is just one way small groups can connect with unchurched people. Some churches have created their own curriculum covering basic spiritual questions related to Christianity. Still others host tough questions forums that allow people to fire off tough spiritual questions. These are all excellent ways to make spiritual connections. Most important to remember is that these types of groups work best when led by seasoned Christians who are well-grounded in God's Word. In addition, it is wise to have a point person over these groups to act as a spiritual coach and adviser.

Letting Go of Preconceived Ideas

If you decide to reach out to the unchurched through small groups, remember that you are taking the church to them. Don't expect them to come to you. Don't be disappointed if they choose to participate in your group but never make a move to become a part of the larger church body. Although that would be ideal, many people may never feel comfortable entering a church building. Your small group may be an expression of church in itself for these people, and this is certainly the trend that many church leaders see today. Be willing to try new things to connect with unchurched people. Not every idea will be successful.

If you fail or only have moderate success, don't give up. Evaluate and analyze what went well and what went wrong. Could you have done anything differently? What did you learn in the process? Were you truly understanding and connecting with the culture or were your efforts counterfeit? People can spot a phony a mile away.

Follow Up to Basic Spiritual Courses

What happens when your study on basic spiritual matters is done? Should your group break up? That is entirely up to you. Some leaders enjoy leading a fresh group of seekers, while others want to take existing groups to the next level. If you decide that it will be a onetime shot, make sure to provide group members with options for learning more about Christ when your study series is over. Suggesting other small groups and providing leader contact information can connect group members with new groups that they can join. Having another leader waiting in the wings to take over group facilitation and continue on is another option.

Unique Groups Related to Culture

Additional affinity groups that may or may not be for seekers include those for students on a college campus, people in prison, military personnel, and those coming from specific denominational backgrounds (for example, Catholics).

Our newspaper recently ran an article about a young man who owned a skateboard shop. The photo showed him sitting cross-legged on the ground while a young skateboarder jumped over him on his board. His interests in his clientele extended far beyond just business interests. He befriended many of the kids who frequented his store. He wanted to be a part of their lives. So he often scheduled video nights and held parties for them as a way of getting into their worlds. His method of relationship-building is a prime example of what the emerging church culture is attempting.

Groups tailored to connect with specific cultures provide a unique link. Such groups may not always have a heavy spiritual emphasis, but they can provide a doorway to discussing spiritual matters should the opportunity arise.

Consider these additional examples of small groups:

- A rural luncheon small group that targets people over 40.
- A moms' group with a parenting course that allows participants to ask questions including spiritual ones. The group hopes to offer a follow-up course introducing Christianity.
- Christian doctors holding healing services after hours.
- A small group in a local restaurant that targets surrounding workplaces and workers.
- After-school clubs and other small-group activities such as those for skateboarders as a way to build bridges to making spiritual connections.
- Craft groups where participants make crafts and participants can receive prayer if needed.

Hundreds of other possibilities for unique small groups abound. Be bold. Try something different. And don't be discouraged if it doesn't turn out as you imagined. God has His own plan, and the end may look totally different from what you expected. Most important is your willingness to try to connect with those outside of the traditional church.

In recent years some have found fault with emerging church cultures, lumping them all into one heap. And I agree that some, in an attempt to connect, have gone too far, bending God's Word to make it more palatable to non-Christ followers. Let me make it clear that that approach is not what I am suggesting.

Stand firm in your faith, using God's Word as your foundation. But look for connecting points to reach these diverse cultures. You may be the only Bible they ever read and your small group the only "church" to which they ever belong. Imagine the effect you could have.

Points to Ponder
Consider Surrounding Cultures

1. What are some of the different cultures you see in your town?

2. How would you define your own lifestyle culture?

3. Brainstorm some ways to connect with the cultures around you.

4. Do any of these give you ideas for small groups? If so, what are they and what do they look like?

part 5

innovation station:
keeping groups energized and fun

12 out of the rut and into the groove

The goal is to "create, capture, and sustain disciples." How can we overcome inertia? To make disciples we need momentum—we must "create, capture, and sustain momentum." So what's the secret? The secret of momentum is to "create, capture, and sustain value."

—Patrick Morley[1]

Mid-February hit and Jan noticed that attendance for her small group had dwindled. They were nearly three-quarters of the way through their chosen study book and even she was weary of the same old thing. Group meetings went something like this: Read the designated scripture passage outlined in the book chapter for the week, ask the questions at the back of the chapter in order, stop and allow room for discussion after each one, have prayer time, eat dessert, and go home. The spark was gone. People weren't as enthusiastic as they once were. What could she do to make the group exciting again?

Keeping Them Coming Back

A set routine for how meetings operate makes group members feel more at ease because they know what to expect. A schedule and a plan make a leader's job much easier too. Just as students need to take a break from the grind of studying, however, small-group members occasionally need to take breaks from the usual curriculum. Groups can become dry and dull after awhile, especially if using the same teaching methods week after week.

Sometimes leaders are so locked into the group routine they overlook how well they connect with members. Members may become tired of the grind and eventually stop coming or show little enthusiasm when they do attend. When interest wanes, attendance often becomes sporadic.

"How can I keep them coming back?" leaders may ask. Here are several suggestions for revitalizing groups.

Varying the Routine

Occasionally changing the way the group studies is one alteration leaders can make. Groups often follow a set routine, and adding additional elements creates more variety. Incorporate other ways to present and discuss the topics you cover. Here are some suggestions: Play a game; watch a film clip that ties into the topic; or use visual aids (object lessons, charts, diagrams, white boards, PowerPoint, etc.).

Ask group members for suggestions. If you find the chosen material no longer holds people's interest, poll members to learn if the problem is because of the subject matter or due to the way the book is being presented.

If the subject matter still interests group members but the method of presentation is the problem, you might want to study other books on the same subject. Or if you feel comfortable, work without the book to create a more interesting way to cover the topic.

Finishing what you start is admirable, and leaders tend to think that if their group begins a book study they must finish it. Sometimes, however, people grow tired of the subject they are studying and are ready to move on. Be flexible enough to wrap things up more quickly if you sense your group is ready to make a change.

Another idea for breathing new life into group routines is to invite a guest speaker. This might be someone who has had firsthand experience with the subject or who has expertise on the topic. For instance, a group studying different religions to help equip its members to connect and share with people of different faiths planned to invite a former Mormon, now a Christian, to come and share about her Mormon experience.

Group members would rather hear from someone who has personally been through the experience than read about it in a book. Guest speakers can also answer group member questions where book studies may occasionally leave some questions unanswered.

Suspending the group topic for a week or so to cover another topic of interest can also reenergize groups. I've participated in small groups where people raised questions about topics during regular studies that they wanted to see covered more in-depth. One small group I belonged to occasionally scheduled something called a Tough Questions Night. On that night members came with tough questions that the group looked up answers to in Scripture and then discussed.

We didn't always end up with tidy answers. Sometimes, after presenting our human, finite understanding based on our grasp of the Bible, the best we could do was leave it up to individual members to reach their own conclusions. Talking about the issues, however, can be an enlightening experience for group members. They not only learn more about the topic but also find that they are not the only ones wrestling with it. Even the most mature Christians grapple with tough issues, so providing a venue where these can be covered is something to consider.

Grouping Your Groups

Varying study methods holds people's interests. Larger groups might consider occasionally organizing members into separate small groups to facilitate discussion. Breakout discussions are beneficial when covering lots of material in a limited time or when a group's large size limits sharing time.

We previously noted that small-group discussion and sharing typically decreases with the size of the group since some shyer members may be intimidated about sharing. Breaking down the group can help members become acquainted with each other and have more time for in-depth discussion. You may want to start the group meeting as a whole and then assign a group discussion leader for each breakout group. Each smaller group can then report back on what they learned after reconvening with the larger group.

Sharing Gatherings

Breakout groups give members more opportunities to share and discuss. You can take a slightly different approach and allow members of your small group to gather with members of other groups. Unlike the group within a group scenario where the purpose is to facilitate discussion, these gatherings can either be for social purposes or to allow a couple of groups to participate in the same study. Occasional intergroup gatherings also help prevent groups from becoming too isolated and cliquish.

Temporarily merging one group with another for a combined group study allows members to learn together. You can make it a onetime event or a series of gatherings depending on the study purpose. Merging a seasoned married couples group with a young-marrieds group to work on marriage enrichment would be one example. Gatherings such as these provide great mentoring opportunities so that those who already have experience can share what they learned with those who have less experience.

Shared gatherings can help group members grow spiritually as they learn from others biblical knowledge and wisdom while hearing about their experiences. Good things can come from group collaboration, but keep these important safeguards in mind:

- First, make sure that you plan well enough and far enough in advance to publicize the shared event to all potential participants. Don't hold last-minute combined gatherings. Your lack of planning will frustrate participants.
- Find a point person to help organize and lead the event or gathering.
- Solicit feedback from group members after the gathering to see what they thought was done well and what needed improvement. Find out if they are open to doing a joint event again in the future.

Turning Study into a Game

Do you need more ideas for shaking up the routine? Try turning study into a game. Our small group had been looking at different religions and their foundational beliefs, comparing them to Christianity. Some of the religions studied thus far included Mormonism, Jehovah's Witnesses, and Judaism.

Debbie, our leader for the evening, decided it would be fun to turn what might have otherwise been a dull learning process into a game. She pulled out exact lines of text from the book and handouts we had studied. Debbie wrote down excerpts on strips of paper that represented a truth or fact about a specific religion or its beliefs. She did this without identifying the religion. For instance, she might have written something like, "Not by grace, but by good works do you enter heaven" or "They do not believe in celebrating birthdays or holidays." She placed these strips into a gift bag and then divided our group into two groups. Then she had a team member draw out a slip of paper and read the belief statement/description aloud.

The team that drew the belief statement received a point if they pinpointed the religion or cult that adhered to that belief. If a team missed, the facilitator gave the other team the opportunity to earn a point. It didn't take long before the members' competitive natures took over. Soon teams were jesting and teasing as members consulted each other, discussing what particular religion the belief belonged to and why. Sometimes teams knew the answers and sometimes they didn't. The leader kept a master list of the beliefs with a key indicating which religion or cult each pertained to.

People loved the game, which was beneficial in several ways.

- It helped group members realize how much they understood.
- It helped them compare and contrast what other religions believed.
- It helped them grasp and commit to memory key foundational beliefs of Christianity and compare them to those of other cults and religions.

The game was so much fun and so useful that members asked to play it again. You can use the same technique and adapt it for other studies. Such games are a great way to refresh and remind members of what they've been learning.

A predictable routine is a definite plus when it comes to small-group leadership, because members come to depend on a leader's reliability. You undoubtedly have favorite product brands you purchase at the store. You buy those products because you know exactly what they will be like. Predictability is often a good thing. But sometimes it can be to your advantage to try new products, because you find new benefits.

Having a set group routine is much like having a favorite product. We know what to expect and there are no unexpected surprises. Routine keeps things running smoothly. But sometimes varying the routine can add variety to gatherings and make them more interesting. One way to do this is to vary how you study and offer additional types of study opportunities. Be on the lookout for signs of restlessness, sagging membership, or lack of interest. If you notice these symptoms, it may be time to stir things up a little with some imaginative changes.

Trying new things can stretch and grow group members. Why not give it a try with your group? You might be pleasantly surprised. We'll look at additional actions you can take to spice up your small group in the next couple of chapters.

Points to Ponder
Ten Signs Your Group Is Becoming Too Predictable

1. Several members treat group meetings like naptimes and have started bringing their pillows and teddy bears.

2. Everyone finishes each other's sentences.

3. Members keep whining, "But all the other groups have them!"

4. Several people have asked, "Didn't we already study this?"

5. Group members have formed teams, are earning immunity, and talk about voting you out of the study.

6. You've had to confiscate several members' cell phones because they keep text messaging each other.

7. Group members pay more attention to the study host's cats than they do to the lesson.

8. Everyone keeps repeating "Yea, verily, yea," after everything you say.

9. If you don't serve milk and cookies at your established meeting conclusion time, members throw tantrums.

10. You've had to hide the TV remote because people keep turning the TV on to *Animal Planet* when you're not looking.

13 innovative ideas for small groups

Consistency is the last resort of the unimaginative.
—Oscar Wilde[1]

Leaders with creative ideas and methods for reaching and teaching small groups establish a learning atmosphere and an almost irresistible climate. People can't wait to come and participate. Innovative techniques keep existing members interested and involved, breathing new life into groups.

Jim Mitchell excels at creative leadership. He is a master at inventing creative approaches to entice, entertain, and equip group participants. Jim leads a Christian men's fellowship in Benicia, California. Though a men's breakfast fellowship sounds like a pretty ordinary group, Jim uses some unique approaches to connect with and teach the men—and they love it.

The Cholesterol Café[2]

Jim's group, the Cholesterol Café, meets at 6:00 every Friday morning at a local waffle shop. Approximately 8 to 12 men attend. One unusual thing about Jim's group is that Jim uses small cards (like business cards) as teaching devices. These often have a zany photo, a whimsical, thought-provoking statement, and a scripture verse that ties in to the message he wants to highlight that day.

Just to give you an idea of Jim's creatively "bent" mind, here's one example of his innovativeness in action. At a recent event hosted by his church to motivate more members to become involved in small groups, Jim had yet another stack of business cards available for potential members. These cards were different from the cards he generates for teaching and are an excellent example of Jim's wry sense of humor. The cards read:

Top 10 Reasons to Attend the Men's Breakfast
10. Duh! Food!
9. Collecting little cards

8. Talking sports

7. Les's Asian jokes (Les, one of the men's breakfast attendees, is a Hawaiian who is always being mistaken for being Asian.)

6. COFFEE

5. Fun e-mails

4. No girlz allowed

3. Movie reviews

2. Real men get up early

1. The Dumpster Train!

One would think such an early time would keep guys from wanting to attend Jim's small group. Some do miss the gathering because they must be at their jobs early. Nor can night owls fathom rising at such an early hour either. For those who do come, however, camaraderie is probably the biggest draw. Most men don't have close personal relationships, but they can feel good about being with a group of guys in a nonthreatening way.

Though outwardly the group may appear unstructured, structure exists. From 6:00 to 6:15 the guys straggle in and, as Jim puts it, "praise God for coffee." For the first 15 minutes or so the guys shake hands and chatter while they try to clear the cobwebs from their brains.

Jim adheres to the familiar adage Keep It Simple Stupid (KISS) for teaching a lesson or Christian principles. He hands out business cards to group members after they have ordered their meals. Each card has a thought on it for discussion plus some scripture. The discussion topic on the card differs from week to week.

Here's a sample card idea that Jim used for one lesson:

The front of the business card has the words "Between the aisle and the window" and the picture of a commercial jet airliner. On the back of the card is the question, "Why do we hate the middle seat? What privileges would you find hard to surrender?" The questions are followed by a scripture verse: "Whoever humbles himself will be exalted" (Matt. 23:12).

The lesson topic is on humility. Jim used this simple method to teach important Christian principles. The guys love the cards because they fit into a wallet and can be carried around as a reminder of what they've learned.

Once the food comes, official lesson time is over. Sometimes the discussion continues on the topic presented, and at other times the men return to discussing sports or something else that has captured their interest.

Jim once completed a short football theme series that included a tabletop competition with the old triangle-shaped paper footballs. You may remember these from your grade school days. Jim presented the winner with a table football trophy, which was a small plastic football player with his arm extended holding a triangular sign that exhibited the year and the words Table Football Champion. The figure stood on a brass candlestick mounted on a small square rectangle painted to look like a football field.

Jim knows that competition (of any kind) can create an adrenaline rush with men, and he shrewdly taps into that. He also recognizes that humor is a great connector and very attractive to most people. He's not afraid to use his own whacky sense of humor to make those connections. The promo card referenced earlier is a key example. Jim mentions the Dumpster train in his top 10 reasons for joining as the number 1 reason for attending the group.

"The Dumpster train is simply a pickup truck pulling at least four Dumpsters (like a train) through the parking lot," Jim explains. "It typically comes around 7 A.M. and has come to signify that the meeting is officially over. It is a little unusual to see, and I must admit that I have never seen it anywhere else. I put it as number 1 as an 'inside joke' but also as the one thing that a guy who has never attended will have to ask about."

Jim also sends out humorous e-mail reminders to group members. The e-mails are just one of the hooks that keep guys coming back. Jim says, "Since being somewhere at 6 A.M. is not the norm for many of these guys, a weekly reminder is necessary. If you can make it humorous, guys will look forward to it. I try to make it relevant to the study or to current events whenever possible."

Jim's group meets every Friday. He sends out e-mail reminders on Wednesdays and these can be rather bizarre. Examples of Jim's reminder e-mails include a picture of the world record holder for shooting milk from his eyeball. Jim put teaser comments in the e-mail to keep guys wondering if their group might try something similar. Another e-mail reminder included a picture of a man who weighed over 1,000 pounds.

That e-mail included a comment about the biscuits and gravy. (Nobody ordered the biscuits and gravy that week.) Sometimes the e-mails create so much excitement among the guys that Jim receives a flurry of "reply all" comments tossed around for the next 36 hours. His e-mail promotion builds enthusiasm for gathering again on Friday.

Jim has a more serious side as well. He recognizes that beneath the lighthearted humor, men are often fearful of letting their guard down. He doesn't push them to do so, but when it happens, he is ready to address whatever questions and issues may arise.

"Men want to spend time with other men but are made to feel guilty if they are not with their wives or kids during their free time," says Jim. "This feeling is subtle, but it is there. Friday morning at 6 A.M. is guilt-free time." Through his creative ideas Jim has successfully established an environment where men can come and safely let their hair down plus learn some biblical foundations in the process.

Jim is the master of innovative approaches, and though the group itself is a pretty standard affair—a Friday morning breakfast—the methods Jim uses keep them coming back. The guys love it. They can hardly wait to roll out of bed on Friday mornings.

A certain amount of fearlessness goes with innovation. Sometimes innovation happens because someone takes an existing idea and simply pushes it one step farther. Sometimes it involves revamping a concept. Innovation can even happen from simplifying a concept. When it comes to small groups, most of us have preconceived ideas of what small groups are, what they look like, and how they operate.

Not everyone is blessed with such a creative mind as Jim Mitchell, but it doesn't mean we can't still be creative with our small groups. When the women's Bible study at Lisa Beamer's church took a summer break, Lisa seized the opportunity to hold a short-term small-group fellowship. Rather than a typical Bible study, Lisa chose to focus on hymns.

For their resources Lisa chose a series called Sing the Faith (published by Augsburg Fortress).[3] This series includes small booklets covering hymns with different themes (prayer, grace, spirituals, etc.). Lisa realized that during the summer months people usually have less time to study. People were very receptive.

"It was really fun," says Lisa. "The nice thing was it required no work at home between sessions. We did everything at the weekly meetings."[4]

Studying the hymns helped group members understand the story and inspiration behind many well-loved Christian songs. Now, when the women sing those songs they have not only a new appreciation for the songs but also a deeper sense of worship.

The Cholesterol Café and its creative use of business cards for short studies and the small-group hymn study are just two innovative ideas for small groups who may want to try something different for a change. You can be innovative with the topic you study, the method by which you choose to study, or even the group's purpose. Reviewing the approaches below may give you ideas for new groups or for adding pizzazz to existing groups.

More Unusual Groups and Methods

Share and care group. Sprouts is the name of both a group and a Bible study curriculum. Sprouts is promoted as a covenant discipleship for young children. The target age is children grades three to six. The children in this small group meet to support each other as they work to live and grow as

Christ's disciples. Sprouts helps teach children and provides suggestions for care-related projects where they not only learn about acts of love but also do acts of love as they work together to help someone in the community.

Through participation, children develop habits of discipleship that will sustain them in their spiritual formation and growth for the rest of their lives. In essence the Sprouts small groups teaches children to put feet on their faith.

Though Sprouts is designed for children, the idea can easily be adapted to groups with a similar purpose, to share basic Christian principles learned through their small discipling group and to care for others by reaching out because of what they have learned. Such groups could form for young adults or even adults.

A group such as the Sprouts group might choose to study a book that emphasizes caring for others and then meet to discuss what members have learned. The group facilitator could then schedule periodic caring activities to give members the opportunity to take what they have learned into the world.

Suggested activities might include a community cleanup day, working at a homeless shelter's food kitchen, and pitching in to help single moms with home maintenance. There are endless possibilities. For more info on the Sprouts curriculum, see our resource section at the end of the book.

Book discussion group. Many libraries and bookstores have small groups that discuss current books. Groups usually meet on a regular basis, choose a specific book (usually a new release) that all of its members read, and then members meet to talk about it.

Sometimes innovativeness is nothing more than the simplification of existing processes and groups. Many Christian small groups already operate similarly to book discussion groups but are more complex because their meetings have more facets.

Regular small-group meetings usually include a discussion of particular scripture passages and prayer. You can simplify Christian small groups to be more similar to book discussion groups. Groups would form for the unique purpose of reading and discussing current Christian book releases. Group members could agree ahead of time about whether the books would be fiction or nonfiction.

Members might wish to read up to a certain point in the book. All that remains is for members to meet and talk about the book—what they liked, what they didn't, and what they felt challenged to do or change in their own lives as a result. The facilitator's only responsibilities are to make certain people know what book they are on, how far they are to read, and where and when the next meeting will occur. These groups, overall, require little maintenance.

Hobby groups. Hobby groups are a specific type of affinity group. Everyone has a hobby. Hobbies might be sports-related, craft-related, writing-related, or something else. The primary focus of hobby groups is to gather people together who enjoy doing and sharing similar interests or activities. The emphasis isn't as much on discipling and learning as it is on the hobby itself. For this reason these types of groups are very appealing to people outside of church. A successful hobby group might include the opportunity for members to gather together and work on similar projects at the same time.

A Christian woman who enjoyed scrapbooking knew many other women enjoyed the same hobby. She decided to form a group and invite other women to meet with her to work on their scrapbooking together. Reminiscent of the old-fashioned quilting bee, the women brought their family photographs and worked on making decorative albums where they creatively displayed their photos. The group didn't incorporate a Bible study, but members shared prayer requests.

Before adjourning, group members shared prayer requests and prayed. The group successfully launched and exploded numerically, growing so quickly that another group sprang from the first group. Perhaps the no-fuss approach the women took was what made it so successful. Their main objective was to have fun, but they also recognized that they could incorporate a spiritual emphasis. Praying for members' needs did not require a special study time or anything else. They could actually share prayer needs while cutting and pasting. All they needed was a little extra time devoted to praying at the end of each session.

Sometimes we make the mistake of thinking that small groups must have a set format with plenty of scriptural study. But not everyone is interested in such a format. Weaving in bits of salt and light into an informal setting can also be a way of discipling and growing members. In addition, it can provide a hook that might draw nonbelievers deeper into a possible relationship with Christ.

Leaders who start hobby groups can find nonintrusive ways to share their Christian perspective. Methods might be as simple as saying, "Would you like to go out for coffee and talk about it?" or "I'll pray for you," when someone in their group shares something that is going on in his or her life. Leaders can look for additional connecting points where they can continue to build bridges with those members. Often it's the little, everyday matters that strengthen the relationships, rather than the grand sweep of things that make a difference in people's lives.

What should you do with the information shared in this chapter? Should you try to launch similar groups and find someone to run them? I wouldn't recommend it. Starting a unique group that you must then find a leader to manage rarely works as successfully as a group that starts because someone with a passion initiated it.

Groups in the latter category are more likely to be successful because they are an exact fit for the interest and talents of the initiator who is at the helm. It was that person's passion that motivated him or her to start the group in the first place.

Looking at the unique examples I've provided can give you ideas for approaches leaders can adapt to their own groups. Sometimes it's just a matter of borrowing bits and pieces of ideas that work and weaving them into what already exists. Plan your curriculum and activities around the natural ages and interests of your groups if you want the maximum effect.

Groups related to age and interests. Gina Maggard leads a group of 6 to 10 middle school children. Gina started the group after her pastor asked if she would consider working with the younger kids in a Sunday School class that included kids 8 to 18 years old. Gina soon found that the group was too broad an age-range to meet the needs of all the kids. So she had to make some adjustments and is now focusing on middle school kids.

Now the small group meets on Wednesday evenings. The kids feel much more at ease with children their own age. The group has a variety of interests. They just finished rehearsing for and performing in an Easter play and are now working on learning sign language to praise and worship songs, which they will perform at a later date.

Karen had worked with her youth group and previous youth groups for years. But she sensed that many of the teen girls she encountered in her present church and community needed a deeper connection where they could be mentored. Her small group sprang from this need. Before long Karen met regularly with her group of 8 to 12 girls. They had a weekly devotional and prayer meeting plus special activities such as slumber parties, attending the latest movies, and other fun activities. Sometimes they planned special service-oriented events.

The girls' parents appreciated Karen because she was often able to make connections with their daughters in ways they could not. Because the girls trusted Karen, they opened up and often shared very private matters. Karen was able to influence them and share God's Word, but she also realized how important it was for the girls to trust that what they shared would remain private.

Other Fun Activities

We have looked at creative approaches for operating and teaching small groups that can help crank up group energy and excitement. Innovativeness doesn't mean you have to launch new groups. Existing groups can also use creative methods for keeping their members engaged at meetings. Here are a few ideas to consider:

If you sense that members are becoming bored with the study, or if you have a few weeks between finishing up one study and starting another, consider holding an Open Forum Night. This is similar to the Tough Questions Night mentioned in chapter 12. Rather than tough questions, have group members suggest biblical topics they would like to discuss ahead of time so you can prepare for them.

Suggested subjects should be something you can cover in one session. For instance, for some reason the Book of Revelation seems to be a popular topic people suggest from time to time. You certainly wouldn't be able to cover the entire Book of Revelation in one sitting.

You could, however, focus on a particular scripture passage that someone suggests for further discussion. Or you might talk about a Christian concept or principle the group has been learning about. Make sure to tell group members that you will not cover every topic and that they need to bring their Bibles so that the group can spend time looking up passages and discussing answers.

You've no doubt heard that imitation is the sincerest form of flattery. If you don't excel at creative ideas, you can still observe and adapt ideas that work in other groups. Learn and borrow from others. Observe what other groups are trying. Listen and swap ideas whenever you can. Apply what you can to your own group, adapting those ideas to meet your group's unique design.

Points to Ponder
Thinking Outside of the Box

1. What unique small groups do you know of that are using an outside-of-the-box method to connect with members or potential members?

2. If you are currently leading a group, list one creative or innovative thing that you might do to spice up your group.

3. Do you have any new ideas after reading this chapter? If so, what were they and how would you adapt them to suit your needs?

14   spicing things up with social events

It can be tough inviting a nonbeliever to our church or Bible study group. But we've found it's easy to invite someone we work with to go out to dinner with our friends.
—Kevin Robertson[1]

We saw in the previous chapter that innovative ideas keep groups fresh. Sometimes, however, it's good to plan activities just for the sake of having fun. Though pleasure is the main purpose, social events also have side benefits.

Tim and Emily* had volunteered in children's ministry for several years but neither had ever participated in a small group before. A small-group ministry promotion made them think more about joining a group, and they asked a friend who they knew to be involved in a group if they had room for one more.

"Sure," their friend said. "Why don't you come and check it out? As a matter of fact, our group leaders are hosting a game night for New Year's Eve. You're welcome to come."

This appealed to Tim and Emily and they came for the evening. They were surprised to learn that they already knew several people at the party. At first Tim, who is quiet and reserved, seemed nervous, but as the evening wore on he jested and joked along with the rest of his team as they tried to outwit their opponents during one of the games. By the end of the evening Tim and Emily had decided they would like to attend the group on a regular basis.

Social events let group members kick back and get acquainted in a relaxed setting. They are also a good way to introduce new potential members to a group. Like Tim and Emily, prospective members socialize with people they may already know or become acquainted with people they haven't previously

---

*Not their real names.

met. Barriers that might otherwise stand in the way of trying out a small group suddenly fall away. People are sometimes hesitant to join a group if they don't know some of its members. If they know a few members even slightly, they are more likely to attend the group's regular gatherings.

Using Members' Gifts

The way in which people join small groups is much like swimming. Some people come to a group and dive right in, while others dabble their toes in the water and wade in slowly. Social events provide a way for new people to wade into a group. Events also create an environment where group members utilize their skills and gifts. We mentioned previously that healthy small groups share a balance of duties and power. This prevents leaders from overtaxing themselves and burning out.

People bring a variety of skills and spiritual gifts with them. Some are naturals at planning extracurricular activities, social events, and even missions and outreach happenings. Those with the spiritual gift of administration frequently help keep order or take on administrative duties because they can't help but implement organization.

Those with the gift of hospitality thrive on making people feel warm and welcome and usually enjoy having people in their homes for special events. People who have a heart for missions or benevolence want to share ideas for helping the less fortunate or reaching non-Christians for Christ. These and other gifts can enrich your group and give joy to members who use them.

Look for ways to incorporate the gifts and passions of group members into your small-group operations. Fun activities provide ample opportunity to use these. Suggest specific dates on which you would like to hold a special event. For instance, in November and December you might want to have your group participate in an outreach activity. You don't necessarily need to plot your group's agenda for the entire year, but pinpointing dates and times for special activities practically guarantees that your group will not become bored with the routine.

You can make a general announcement asking group members to volunteer, or personally ask group members who have gifts most suited to the event to help make the event a reality.

Members cherish and remember fun activities. One of the easiest gatherings to plan and execute is the good old-fashioned cookout. Burgers and chips are delicious, but if this is too ordinary for you, then dare to be a bit more creative.

When planning your event, be sensitive to the financial standing of group members. Some members have more expendable income than others. Don't plan events that will cause members with financial struggles to either over-spend or skip the event due to budget constraints. Try to plan gatherings everyone can attend.

One solution to members' tight finances is to offer a scholarship to group members who might want to attend special events but cannot afford the full cost. You can ask members to contribute to this fund, explaining the fund's purpose. Setting your fee, if there is one, a few dollars above what you would normally ask can also provide the funds you need. Use this extra money for the scholarship, or you may simply make the event free of charge.

For the sake of privacy, the contributing members do not need to know who received the scholarship nor do those asking for assistance need to make it known. Mention to your members that a scholarship is available should any-one need additional assistance.

Here are a few ideas for social events that different groups have put into practice.

A Zillion Ideas for Social Events

Movie night. Gather members together to watch a video. Most everyone enjoys going to the movie theater; the downside is that you can't actually talk during a movie (unless you enjoy getting shushed by the members of the audi-ence) and that leaves little opportunity for socializing.

If you want members to socialize, watching a movie at a theater might not be the best choice. If you do choose to go to the movies, you might include eating out before or after the show so people have a chance to connect. Other types of movie nights include:

- **Movies with a message.** You can show DVDs of movies that have moral, life value messages, or character growth principles for discussion. Some movies that come to mind that would be appropriate include the Lord of the Rings trilogy (obviously not a good choice for just one night), *Les Miserables, Life Is Beautiful,* or *Amazing Grace.*

  Sometimes it is difficult to find films without offensive language, vio-lence, or sexual content. You can actually rent edited films from compa-nies that clean up the films for more general viewing. One such organiza-tion is cleanfilms.com, which edits films for language, violence, and sexual content.

- **Cheesy monster movie night.** A small group combined a burger cook-out with a corny monster movie night. The event took place near Hal-loween, so the group chose monster movies for their viewing pleasure. But not just any monster movie would do. They deliberately chose the corniest 1950s monster movie they could find. *The Creeping Terror* brought plenty of laughs. The group carried the 1950s theme through the entire event, and the burgers and hotdogs tied in nicely. Someone even volunteered to make milkshakes for everyone at the soda shop.

- **Movie marathon.** A church held a caroling party for its teens, who then returned to the church for a Christmas movie marathon. Teens sacked out on the floor with their favorite quilts and sleeping bags and watched some of their favorite movie classics while munching on Christmas goodies. You can easily adapt movie marathon night to a small group as a fun family event for any season.

Take me out to the ball game. One of the small groups at my church occasionally attends professional baseball games as a social event. It helps add to the fun if your local team is red hot and doing well. Unlike going to the movie theater, baseball gives people the opportunity to talk while they watch or, if they prefer, scream and shout (hopefully not at each other). Spectator games such as baseball are a great way to become more familiar with each other and find out who the real sports fanatics are.

Play ball. How about a friendly game of softball, basketball, or football? Softball in particular is a fun coed sport. You don't, however, want overly competitive members to cause hurt feelings. So you may have to coach to make sure participants keep the game friendly. If you have members who are extremely competitive, this might not be the best choice for a social activity.

Go camping. Not everyone enjoys camping, but some small groups have planned successful camping outings and really enjoyed the back-to-nature experience. The time spent around a campfire or on a hiking trail together can create lifetime memories.

Weekend getaway. Renting a beach house or cabin (or cabins) for the weekend is another great event. Our small group rented a large beach house on the Pacific Ocean at Bodega Bay over Father's Day weekend.

Multiple families under one roof quickly taught us about each others' quirks. But we had great fun. The last day of the event we had our own seafood fest and cooked fresh crabs, scallops, and salmon on the grill. I'll never forget the hysterical picture we snapped of Dave, one of our more experienced coastal members holding a crab in each hand with a wide grin on his face. Dave and James showed us how real men cook and eat seafood that weekend.

Girls' night out/Boys' night in. Planning a time where group members of the same gender can go out for a good time is also fun. Even more to be treasured are same-gender events that allow parents to escape parenting responsibilities. Sometimes parents desperately need a break.

One spring, a group of women from a small group planned a getaway to the city. They drove to San Francisco where they visited a Degas exhibit at the San Francisco art museum, then attended a concert at a local cathedral. They topped off the evening with dessert at a favorite restaurant.

Guys don't seem to need the bonding time as much as women, and they're more likely to want to stay home, sacked out on the couch with the remote control, but they can still schedule in some fun events. Another small group I know of regularly had guys over for football and food during football season, and it became a popular event for the men (although women weren't excluded).

Game night. Game night is the perfect small-group event when cost is a factor. You need only pay for the snacks. I know of several small groups that hold game nights on New Year's Eve. You can hold game nights any time of year. You will have to decide if you want to include entire families or just couples. Ask everyone to bring their favorite food and game. Depending on how many people show up, you can either divide into separate groups and go into different rooms to play different games or spend the evening as one large group playing a variety of games.

Murder mystery dinner. Do you love a mystery? You can choose several ways to present a murder mystery. The easiest way is to watch the local newspaper for murder mystery dinner theaters and then make reservations as a group. You can also, however, plan your own event.

There are many different murder mystery party games available. You can even have one custom-designed for you. During the event a murder is either acted out or guests arrive at the event to find a murder has occurred. Each person assumes a role for the evening and must help solve the murder. A variety of choices exist. Areyougame.com has prepackaged murder mystery games. Several combined groups at our church utilized a murder mystery created by Dinnerandamurder.com, and it was great fun. They offer a choice of numerous themes and game sizes and even include the option of having a game custom-made. In addition, they even have fund-raiser games.

One final option for murder mystery dinners is to actually bring in actors to mingle among dinner guests. Murder mystery dinners of this nature take a bit more planning, since actors must rehearse a part. If you want this type of murder mystery, talk with friends and acquaintances who participate in drama. Your local high school, youth group, community theater, or church drama group (if you have one) are a good resource. Or you might check with local groups who perform in murder mystery dinner theaters to see if they are willing to perform at yours.

Actors love an audience. Some might even perform for free if you are willing to feed them.

Concerts. If you are fortunate enough to live in a geographic area with many special event opportunities, your group members might enjoy attending concerts together. The biggest challenge is to find a concert or performance that will suit everyone's tastes. The cheapest way is to check with area churches to find out about visiting performers they may have lined up. Larger churches sometimes schedule performances by lesser-known artists. These concerts are free or at minimal cost.

Christian radio stations frequently promote regional concerts by more well-known artists. The general rule is that the less well known the artist is, the cheaper the tickets. Musicians who have not yet reached the fame level of more well-known celebrities may be just as talented.

Sometimes the price of attending regional Christian gatherings includes large concerts. These often draw many large-name artists, and though they may cost more, you get more bang for the buck. Events like Fish Net on the East Coast and Spirit West Coast on the West Coast are some that come to mind. And here's something else your group might want to consider.

Many of these large events need plenty of extra help. To host that many people, they need volunteers. If you plan well enough in advance, you can volunteer to help as a group and enjoy the music and speakers at no cost. Your group has the opportunity to serve while contributing to their own spiritual growth. What a deal!

Celebration time. Celebration gatherings are special-event nights that use any combination of worship, drama, special music, videos, and a special message based on a monthly theme. Following the celebration, those attending are invited to the foyer for refreshments and live music.

Coffee, tea, and . . . fellowship. Every other Friday night a singles' group combines their group meetings into a coffeehouse format. People are invited to come and enjoy Christian music in a relaxing, nonthreatening environment. Those who attend are welcome to refreshments and lively discussions. Maybe your group would enjoy having a similar format that combines entertainment with fellowship.

Boccie battle. Over Labor Day weekend a small-group leader invited group members and their families over for a cookout. Group leaders asked everyone to bring a side dish in addition to the hot dogs, hamburgers, and drinks provided by the hosts. The after-dinner entertainment consisted of breaking in a new boccie set, which the host had purchased just for the event.

If you are not familiar with boccie, it is best described as a game somewhere between pool and croquet. The lawn game is played with heavy balls that are slightly larger than croquet balls. The object of the game is to nudge as close to the target ball as possible without hitting it.

Members divided up into teams and the battle was on. In this case the men and women competed, and unfortunately for the men, the women won. The fun family event allowed all ages to participate, and a new boccie tradition was started. The men are anxious for a rematch.

Wedding rewind. A small group in Michigan planned a special event inviting couples in the group to participate in a potluck dinner and evening of reflection on their marriages. In addition to sharing a dish, leaders asked couples to bring memorabilia and photos of their courtship and/or wedding, then asked members to share about how they met their mates. Afterward they held a short prayer service for group members and their marriages.

Progressive dinner. If you haven't done this, you've really got to give it a try. Progressive dinners are not for the Christmas season only, though that's often when people choose to have them. If you are unfamiliar with progressive dinners, they operate something like this: The group starts out at one house where they are served an appetizer, then moves on to the next house where members might have a salad, then on to the next house for the main course, and they finally conclude with dessert. The host at each home is generally the one who prepares the course served at the home. Those not hosting at their homes can assist the host families with food preparation.

Take a hike. Adventurous sorts can plan a hike and a breakfast. One small group did this, meeting at a specific time at a designated recreation center. They divided up by groups and chose selected trails based on the mileage those in their group felt they could handle. One group hiked over a mile, another about 2.5 miles, and the third went over 4 miles.

Hikers returned to a pavilion for fresh cooked omelets, fruit, muffins, and juice. (Less adventurous types might volunteer to stay behind and cook the meal.) Hiking is a great opportunity to bring several small groups together or invite non-Christians to come and socialize. You never know where it may lead!

Hawaiian luau. Two groups decided to combine for an end-of-the-season celebration. They hosted a luau at one of the group member's homes and invited members and their families. A group member assigned people different tropical dishes to bring. Entertainment included limbo, goofy Hawaiian-themed relay races complete with hula hoops, and a Christian Hawaiian dance group who performed several dances and then taught the men and women one dance each.

The group hadn't anticipated giving away prizes for costumes, but they couldn't resist after one burly male group member showed up in Hawaiian garb consisting of a coconut brassiere and grass skirt. He upstaged the Hawaiian dancers!

Sound the retreat. Scheduling a weekend retreat or a weeklong retreat can serve several purposes for small groups. Retreats provide members an opportunity to get away from the rat race and focus on more spiritual matters, as well as draw group members together. Retreats can create a prime environment for rest and refreshment. They are also an ideal way to gather, train, and revitalize leaders.

A women's small group held a weekend retreat in an area known for its spas. The group enjoyed pampered treatment and delicious meals but also worked in time for spiritual renewal. The group leader sent members off to nearby trails and nature areas to spend an hour by themselves.

One woman said, "When I first heard our leader say an hour, I thought, 'What am I going to do for an hour by myself?' Then I went off and found a beautiful spot by a brook and spent time talking with God. I was surprised at how fast the time went and how refreshed and peaceful I felt at the end. Several other women had the same reaction and all were amazed afterward at what a positive and renewing time it was." The group can't wait to do it again next year.

Special events can be enjoyable for small-group members. Holding one or two events a year gives much-needed and much-appreciated time for group member socialization. Be sure to allow time periodically at group meetings to discuss the possibilities of small-group gatherings. You might be surprised by the ideas that surface, and the events will be a memorable time for all.

Points to Ponder
Social Event Planning Guide

Use the space below to brainstorm special events you might want to plan for your small group. Remember to take into account all group members' likes and dislikes and not just your own.

1. List some common interests some of the people in your group have. (Not every member will have a common thread; however, several may.)

2. Check any of the following suggestions in which you think group members might like to participate:
   ☐ combined group studies
   ☐ combined outreach events
   ☐ movie night; ☐ movies with a message; ☐ monster movie night
   ☐ ball games: ☐ spectators; ☐ playing
   ☐ murder mysteries
   ☐ hiking
   ☐ camping

3. List any ideas for special events not listed above that small-group members might enjoy.

4. How many special social events you would like to have per year?

Circle the months in which you think you should have these events.

Jan.   Feb.   Mar.   Apr.   May   June   July   Aug.   Sept.   Oct.   Nov.   Dec.

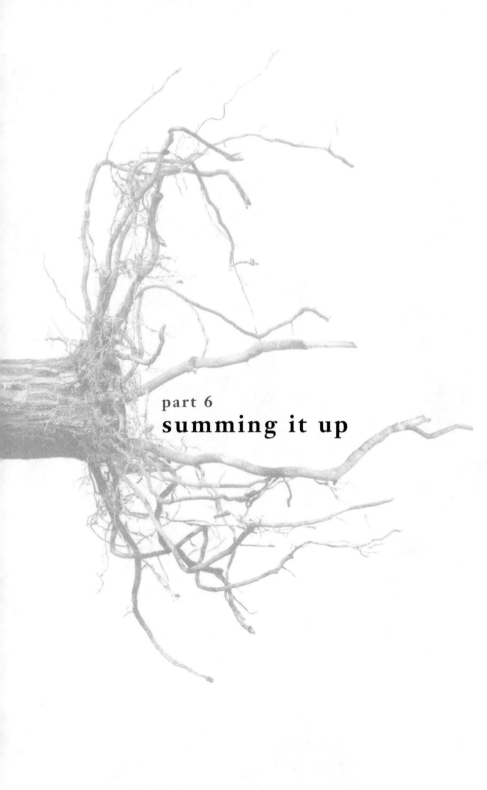

part 6
summing it up

15 life-changing small groups

We have been in small group men's/women's Bible studies
and a Thursday night Bible study with our church . . . but
our greatest passion is small group marriage Bible studies
and meeting couple to couple. We are passionate about
the resurrection power of Jesus Christ in marriage.
—Monique Woodward[1]

Our church, like many others, has discovered that people's personal stories are
one of the most powerful evangelization tools. Every month or so we ask
someone to share how his or her life has been transformed through Christ. I've
noticed a pattern with these testimonials. Time after time, those who share talk
about their small-group connection, how the group became their family, and
how through the love and encouragement of group members they found a lifeline to help them hang on.

Those of us in ministry are in the business of changing lives, but we have
limits to how much energy we can expend. Small groups do what leaders
alone can't do—and often much more effectively.

One Sunday morning Doug* told his story to our congregation. In recent
years his life had mirrored that of Job's in the Bible. Everything that could go
wrong did go wrong. His wife falsely accused him of abusing both herself and
their children, and the stir she caused resulted in Doug losing his job, being
arrested, and having his children taken away from him. He lost everything.
The bail bond was set so high that he could not even make bail.

When he was finally released from jail, he was at rock bottom. Jobless,
childless, and penniless, he didn't even have a bike for transportation. Doug
reached out to the only source he could think of—a church. He made a connection with a member named John who listened to Doug's story. John took
time out of his busy schedule to pick Doug up and bring him to the church

---

*Not his real name.

services. Doug became involved in a men's small group and later in a recovery group. He became a Christ follower because of the outpouring of love he'd experienced through the church's ministry.

Today he has a good job and full custody of his children. His ex-wife's charges have been proven false, and she has since been diagnosed with mental illness. If it weren't for the caring people in the church community and the small groups who gave him a safe place to recover and grow, it's hard to say where Doug would be today.

Kay's husband died more than a decade ago. Last year several women in her church lost their spouses unexpectedly. Kay knew she had to do something and that something was to provide a support network for grieving spouses. She had never done it before but was willing to try.

Today her group has 12 members. One of the members who had just lost his wife told Kay and the other members, "I wish we'd never met," meaning that if it hadn't been for the loss of a spouse he would never have needed such a group. He went on to say, "I don't know what I would have done without this group." The group has been a lifeline that has helped this man and others climb out of the black pit of despair.

Jack* became a small-group leader when his group multiplied. The leader asked if he and his wife would facilitate a group. Though he was a young Christian and had never led a group before, the leader could already see that Jack was growing spiritually, soaking up whatever biblical instruction he could find. He knew Jack was leadership material.

Today Jack's group is thriving, and he continues to develop his shepherding skills to care for his little flock. He has also gained confidence and is becoming involved in other leadership aspects of his church. His small group supports each other through prayer, and Jack has mentored and coached one member whose marriage is experiencing turmoil. Though this member's marriage is going through some rough times, he remains firmly committed to Christ and working things out with his marriage partner. The steadfast resolve to press on toward the goal can be attributed to Jack's leadership and the group's spiritual and physical support during the crisis.

Johnny, a youth leader, wanted to disciple some of the teens in the youth group. He chose a handful of young men with whom he'd developed relationships and invited them to join him every Monday night for dinner and a Bible study. The guys took turns cooking dinner. Sometimes they had macaroni and cheese, sometimes hot dogs, sometimes they had to throw out the dinner and order a pizza.

---

*Not his real name.

Johnny's discipling paid off. He encouraged kids that might otherwise have grown lukewarm in their faith to keep reading and studying their Bibles. Several have gone on to some other type of Christian ministry or leadership involvement, all because one person felt he should spend a little time to take some young men to a deeper level.

Applying the One Another Commands

Small groups exemplify what it means to be a part of God's family. Members learn to sincerely care about one another while setting aside the me-first attitudes and developing humility and sacrificial giving. Scriptures list over 20 "one another commands." God gave these commands to model how we should treat one another. Many small groups are unaware they are already putting these one another commands into practice. By doing so, the church body can flourish and grow to maturity. You can find a list of most of these commands at the Ministry Tools Resource Center Web site <http://mintools.com/bodylife4.htm>. Below are some examples. Notice how well they apply to small groups.

> **Accept one another:** "Accept one another, then, just as Christ accepted you, in order to bring praise to God" (Rom. 15:7). . . .
>
> **Forgive one another:** "Be kind and compassionate to one another, forgiving each other, just as in Christ God forgave you" (Eph. 4:32). . . .
>
> **Love one another:** "Let no debt remain outstanding, except the continuing debt to love one another" (Rom. 13:8).[2]

When Christ followers put these commands into practice, the impact is far-reaching. An excellent illustration of this is found Acts 4:32-35. Those made new in Christ reflected His Christlike qualities as they merged together in groups of caring believers exemplifying obedience to these commands: "All the believers were one in heart and mind" (v. 32). The chapter goes on to talk about how everyone shared their possessions so selflessly that there were no needy people among them. Imagine the difference this would make to people's needs if everyone banded together in small groups such as this.

When people network needs and care for each other as family, we gain a glimpse of heaven and the way God truly means for His children to live. Small groups teach people to put others before themselves.

The Process of Becoming

The apostle Paul wrote to the Philippians, "In all my prayers for all of you, I always pray with joy because of your partnership in the gospel from the first day until now, being confident of this, that he who began a good work in you will carry it on to completion until the day of Christ Jesus" (Phil. 1:4-6).

What better environment exists for allowing Christ's love to be exhibited and for developing mature Christians. Small groups are a training ground for learning how to be godly men and women. They are a safe refuge for the wounded and an outlet for sharing life experiences. Groups serve as inspiration for caring, serving, and giving as well as an environment for developing leaders.

Small groups embody the one another commands that mirror God's desire for how we should relate to Him and care for one another. By working to launch and develop small groups and small-group facilitators, we equip the Kingdom to reach others for Christ while encouraging them to press on toward the goal. People who experience small-group community come to participate in the ultimate power of transformation. Small groups provide a sweet taste of what the Kingdom will be like when we move into eternity.

If one were to sum up the essence of small groups in one word, that word would be *becoming*. Small groups place people into the active role of becoming what God wants them to be.

We are works in process. Together, through this unique form of community with other fallible humans and connectedness with God, we can continue to press on toward the goal, allowing God to carry the good work He began in us on to completion.

Points to Ponder
What Is God Asking You to Do?

1. After reading this book, has your sense of direction and perception of small groups changed? If so, how?

2. If you could launch any kind of small group or small-group program, what would it look like? Use the space below to brainstorm ideas.

3. Look at the groups you brainstormed above. Put a star by the idea that is most appealing to you. If there are several, then choose the one you think will either have the most impact or will be easiest to launch. Pray over the idea and ask someone else you trust to pray for your decision regarding this group; then follow your heart.

appendix
small-group resources

recovery ministry facilitator agreement

As a facilitator of _____ (recovery ministry name) I understand my role is to work with participants to help them identify and overcome hurts, habits, and hang-ups so that they can work toward a healthy existence. I will utilize Christ's principles and God's Word to guide participants and will apply them in my own life to set a godly example.

I realize that recovery ministry is not a counseling ministry. Therefore, I will not offer counsel but will share from my own life experiences and those of others to support and encourage participants. In addition, I plan to intercede for these members via prayer, to help them heal and grow toward Christian maturity.

Any information a participant shares with me will remain confidential and can only be discussed with other recovery facilitators in this church's ministry. If I wish to share this information with someone outside of _____ _____ (church name/recovery group name), I will first obtain permission from the one who shared it before discussing it elsewhere.

I will do my best not to hinder the healing of group participants by forcing my own personal assumptions, insight, or thinking on them. I will seek to help participants have a genuine encounter with Jesus Christ and will use the example of Christ's life and His teachings as a foundation for healing.

If I find that an individual's problems are beyond my skills so that he or she requires a trained and qualified professional, I will seek the advice of my supervisor and will make referrals when deemed necessary.

Name _____

Date _____

Supervisor's Name _____

recovery ministry participant agreement

As a participant in _____ (recovery ministry name) I agree to work with my facilitator and other participants to identify and overcome my hurts, habits, and hang-ups so that I can work toward a healthy lifestyle.

I realize that this recovery ministry is not a counseling ministry. Therefore I will not hold the church, group members, or the facilitator liable for advice given therein.

I understand that any information shared with the facilitator(s) or other participants will remain confidential. If I wish to share this information with someone who is not a participant in this program within this church, I will first obtain permission from the one who shared it before discussing it elsewhere.

I will do my best not to hinder the healing of other group participants by forcing my own personal assumptions, insight, or thinking on participants or facilitators.

If I find that my hurts, habits, or hang-ups are beyond my skills or those of the group facilitator(s) or participants, I will not hold them responsible but will seek the advice of a professional counselor.

Name _____

Date _____

small-group resources

The following are small-group resources for small-group leaders, including those who facilitate affinity groups. Resources include suggested books and studies for small groups.

General Small-Group Leader Resources (Nonbook)

Discipleship Journal. Includes scripturally based articles and studies that are excellent for discipling or small-group study. The DJ Plus section in the back of the magazine covers ideas for small groups, leadership, and other ministries. *Discipleship Journal* is published by NAV Press, which also produces Bible studies specifically designed for small groups <http://www.navpress.com/Magazines/DJ>.

DreamBuilders Ministry in Motion. Provides ministry tips and encouragement resources for pastors, volunteers, and church leaders and a free ministry-related e-zine. The e-zine runs book reviews, and many of these books are appropriate for small-group study, leader equipping, and spiritual maturity. The site is organized by ministry specific focuses, and each ministry category includes recommended resources that can be ordered via the Web site <http://www.ministryinmotion.net>.

Smallgroups.com. This Web site is dedicated entirely to small groups. The site offers an e-zine and resources for small groups, including a CD with the best of article topics their e-zine has covered <http://www.smallgroups.com>.

Christianitytoday.com/smallgroups. *Christianity Today's* Web site has a great archive of articles and resources dedicated to small groups <http://www.christianitytoday.com/smallgroups>.

Upper Room. Upper Room ministries focus is on prayer, devotional, and small-group resources <http://upperroom.com/bookstore>.

Small-Group Leader Resources (Book)

Leading Life-Changing Small Groups, revised by Bill Donahue (Zondervan, 2002). Information, practical tips, and insights that will teach your leadership team about small-group philosophy and structure, discipleship, conducting meetings, and more. You can order this book from your local Christian bookstore or by visiting their Web site <http://ministryinmotion.net>.

Building and Growing Your Small Group Ministry, by Judith M. Bunyi (Discipleship Resources, 2002). Bunyi's book provides a biblical and theological starting point for small-group ministry, plus benefits and challenges of small-group ministry. You'll find all the necessary foundational elements to help you start and maintain small-group ministry. The book also includes strategies to help existing groups improve effectiveness.

Growing People Through Small Groups, by David Stark and Betty Veldman Wieland (Bethany House, 2004). Stark and Wieland's book takes a principles-based approach to small-group ministry. No one-size-fits-all model exists. Learn how to establish a small group rooted in God's will in relation to the specific message and vision of your church. Sociological principles serve as the foundation to the life and development of the small group.

Building a Church of Small Groups: A Place Where Nobody Stands Alone, by Bill Donahue and Russ Robinson (Zondervan, 2001). Donahue and Robinson pull from their small-group leadership experience at Willow Creek Church (a church of 18,000). Learn the vision, values, and steps needed to integrate small groups into your church ministry.

The Serendipity Bible—NIV for Personal and Small Group Study (Zondervan, 1996). A Bible specially designed for small-group study. Perfect for study leaders and members. This Bible includes thought-provoking discussion questions on scripture passages.

Experiencing Discipleship: A Small Group Faith-Building Adventure, by Clarence Shuler (Group Publishing, 2002). A useful tool for bringing your small-group members to a deeper level of spiritual maturity.

Resources for Leading Affinity Groups

Evangelism/Seeker Groups

Alphausa.org or Alphacanada.org. Resources to help people explore spirituality from a Christian perspective. "No question is considered too simple or too hostile."

Seeker Small Groups: Engaging Spiritual Seekers in Life-Changing Discussions, by Gary Poole (Zondervan, 2003). This book won both the Silver Medallion Book Award and the 2004 Christianity Today Book Award of Merit. Poole provides a thorough account of how to launch a seeker small group in a wide variety of settings.

Recovery Groups

Celebrate Recovery. Saddleback Church developed the Celebrate Recovery curriculum and books to promote self-respect, strength, and healing from a Christian perspective for those who have been involved in self-destructive behavior, life struggles, and addictions. Based on the Beatitudes, the teaching tool developed by Rick Warren and John Baker offers a structured, fellowship-based program. Many additional recovery resources have been developed since the initial curriculum was printed. You can find these at <http://www.ministry-inmotion.net> or at <http://www.pastors.com>.

Parenting Groups

A Gift from God, Foundational Principles of Biblical Parenting, by Larry Mercer (Moody, 2001). This is an excellent guide for raising children with a biblical foundation. A workbook, which is great for group study, is also available.

Women's Ministry

The Complete Women's Ministries Kit, by Janelle R. Parker (Beacon Hill Press of Kansas City, 2007). This resource not only outlines how to begin and maintain a women's ministry but also includes 100 program ideas. The kit comes complete with a CD containing modifiable and printable forms, full-size patterns for craft projects, and sample brochures and flyers.

Women's Ministry Handbook, by Carol Porter (Victor, 1992). This handbook covers the wide range of practical information you need for starting a women's ministry: choosing leaders (including spiritual gifts and temperament tests), organizing Bible studies, discipling others, and planning retreats. You can find this at <http://www.ministryinmotion.net/ministry_women.html>.

Designing Effective Women's Ministry, by Jill Briscoe, Laurie Katz McIntyre, Beth Seversen (Zondervan, 1995). Tips and techniques for successful women's ministry from the authors who have vast experience in women's ministry.

Men's Ministry

The Complete Men's Ministries Kit, by Stan Toler and Jerry Brecheisen (Beacon Hill Press of Kansas City, 2007). Here are the resources and ideas you need for starting and equipping a men's ministry. The topics covered in this kit range from promotion and maintenance to spiritual formation, mentoring, and outreach. A 12-week group Bible study is also included. The resource CD that comes with the kit contains modifiable and printable forms, sample posters, and other program pieces.

How to Build a Life-Changing Men's Ministry, by Steve Sonderman (Bethany House, 1996). Help the men in your congregation become what God wants them to be by mobilizing a powerful men's ministry. Sonderman shows you how! A full-time men's pastor, he gives you the nuts and bolts for assembling an on-fire program. Learn to plan strategically, build effective leadership, develop healthy small groups, and expand missions and outreach.

Effective Men's Ministry: The Indispensable Toolkit for Your Church, by Phil Downer (Zondervan, 2001). Written by experienced national leaders from the

National Coalition of Men's Ministries (a partnership of over 75 ministries from over 30 denominations), this book is intended as a guide for churches wishing to start ministries for men. The book has 26 chapters that show how to plan, organize, and lead an effective men's ministry.

Children's Ministry

Sprouts. Sprouts curriculum targets children ages three to six and uses discipling methods via small groups to teach children caring and reaching out to show that care to others. Developed by the United Methodist Church, the material covers how to start a Sprouts group, plans for training leaders, helps for leading the weekly Sprouts meetings, and reproducible resources for publicizing groups and keeping parents, leaders, and children involved. You can find this and other small-group resources at <http://www.upperroom.org>. Go to their bookstore link, and then key Sprouts into their search box for the most up-to-date version.

Single Adult Ministry

Single Adult Ministry for Today, by Bobbie Reed (Concordia, 1996). The complete manual for successful single adult ministry. Contemporary and suited for eager novice leaders and for experienced leaders who are training new team members. Bobbie Reed has over 21 years experience in singles ministry as a lecturer, speaker, consultant, and small-group leader.

Groups for Those with Chronic Illness

Restministries.org. Rest Ministries is a Christian organization for people who live with chronic illness or pain. They offer resources, free daily devotionals, plus a small-group program called HopeKeepers. They will give you a free info pack on starting a HopeKeepers group. Contact Rest Ministries, P.O. Box 502928, San Diego, CA 92150 (888-751-7378) <Restministries.org>.

Recommended Books and Resources for Small-Group Study

Resources suitable for small groups abound. Those listed below are ones I have personally screened and recommend. There are many more books available.

Books

The Sermon on the Mount: LifeGuide Topical Bible Study, by John Stott (Inter-Varsity Press, 2000). A study that looks at Jesus' sermon on the mount and what it means to seek God's kingdom first. Includes leader notes.

The Jesus Touch: Learning the Art of Relationship from the Master, by Lynn Anderson (Howard, 2002). Jesus is available, sensitive, helpful, and creative. This book shows us how to relate better to others by learning from Jesus' example.

The author/speaker draws from Jesus' encounters with individuals, each with his or her own unique history and needs. Each chapter includes a first-person account of the event, told from the eyes of those who were involved, followed by the scripture passage that shows how the event unfolded.

Chapters focus on familiar stories, such as the woman at the well, the wedding miracle in Cana, the feeding of the 5,000, Nicodemus, Paul at the Areopagus, and more. Every chapter concludes with a Creative Touch section and thought questions to make us reflect on our own experiences with that particular theme and action questions to encourage us to put what we've learned into practice. A great book to read on your own or to use for small-group study.

The Purpose-Driven Life: What on Earth Am I Here For? by Rick Warren (Zondervan, 2002). What does it mean to live a life of purpose? Pastor Rick Warren leads you through an insightful look at what it is to understand your God-designed purpose and how to fulfill that purpose as you go about your daily life. Order from your local Christian bookstore or through <http://www.ministryinmotion.net/church_purpose_driven.html>.

God Came Near, by Max Lucado (Multnomah, 1987). Written in a fluid, lyrical, and easy-to-grasp style that shows Lucado's obvious giftedness as a writer. His unique and original perceptions of Christ/God gleaned from his own study of Scripture couple with his life experiences for a warm and inviting book that challenges you as a Christ follower to think about Christ/God's divinity and humanity. Even the most mundane things, like the birth of Christ in a stable, which we are so familiar with, becomes magical and fresh as Lucado explores how God humbled himself to become human for our sakes. Suitable for those wishing to grow in Christian maturity, the book includes study questions in the back with observations and questions that are useful for small-group Bible studies.

Foundations: 11 Core Truths to Build Your Life On Curriculum Kit, by Kay Warren and Tim Holladay (Zondervan, 2002). Developed by Saddleback teachers Kay Warren and Tom Halladay, this purpose-driven curriculum helps maturing believers see the world, their lives, and their spirituality through the filter of God's truth. The kit includes 24 sessions that cover the biblical perspectives about God, Jesus, the Holy Spirit, Revelation, Creation, Salvation, Sanctification, Good and Evil, the Afterlife, and the Second Coming. The complete kit includes two separate leader's guides, one participant's guide, and PowerPoint slides for each session on a CD-ROM. Order through your Christian Bookstore or through <http://www.ministryinmotion.net/church_purpose_driven.html>.

People of Purpose, by Teena Stewart (Ministry in Motion, 2004). This 12-lesson study can be used for independent study or group study of spiritual gifts, abilities and skills, and life experience. People of Purpose is an excellent study for helping members see how they are uniquely designed and the possibilities of where to use their gifts and skills to serve Christ. The book gives examples of people with each gift and includes TIO (Try It Out) ministry opportunities. Available through <http://www.ministryinmotion.net>.

God in You, by Dr. David Jeremiah (Multnomah, 2000). Many Christians remain baffled by the Holy Spirit and have difficulty grasping the Spirit's purpose and power. Dr. Jeremiah breaks the concept of the Holy Spirit into bite-size, digestible chunks for nonacademics. The book's 15 chapters are devoted to such topics as the attributes of the Holy Spirit, what it means to be born of the Spirit, what it means to be filled with the Spirit, the gifts of the Spirit, the fruit of the Spirit and how the Spirit can fill and control church members, marriages, families, workplaces, and lives. Each chapter is backed with a thorough research of Scripture. Though it is not in curriculum format, the book is user-friendly, written in easy-to-understand language, and can easily be used for individual or small-group study. Order at your local Christian bookstore or by visiting <http://www.ministryinmotion.net/bible_studies.html>.

To Serve with All Your Strength, by Fran Sciacca (NavPress, 2000). An insightful and in-depth look at 10 attributes of Christians through Scripture and study of biblical examples such as Nicodemus, Solomon, the unnamed man of Luke 12:13-15, Aquila and Priscilla, Titus, Job, Rehoboam, the unjust steward of Luke 16:1-15, Paul, and the Good Samaritan. Each chapter has an Abiding Principle and a quote to focus the lesson, a Snapshot synopsis, scripture study, recap, application questions with additional scripture, and suggested memory verses. Order at your local Christian bookstore or by visiting <http://www.ministryinmotion.net/bible_studies.html>.

Four-Dimensional Jesus: Seeing Jesus Through the Eyes of Matthew, Mark, Luke, and John, by John Timmer (Faith Alive Christian Resources, 2001). See Jesus through the eyes of Matthew, Mark, Luke, and John. The writers of the four Gospels were not biographers but interpreters of the Good News. This study, divided into 13 sessions, uses spiritual giants such as Dietrich Bonhoeffer, C. S. Lewis, and Eugene H. Peterson to add depth while exploring and comparing each Gospel. Order at your local Christian bookstore or through <http://www.ministryinmotion.net/bible_studies.html>.

Scripture Study Resources

Biblegateway.com is a Web site where you can research scripture passages in a variety of translations <http://www.biblegateway.com>.

Blueletterbible.org is an excellent resource for studying the original translation and the meaning and nuances of words and scripture passages <http://www.blueletterbible.org>.

Other Resources

Tough Questions <http://www.gotquestions.org/bookstore1.html>. This Web site is dedicated to answer tough questions that seekers, new Christians, and even established Christians may have. If your group wishes to study tough questions as a group, ample books on a related topic abound.

Weekly Willow Creek Small-Group Curriculum <http://www.willow-creek.org/life_curriculum.asp>. Willow Creek church has over 18,000 attendees. They upload a weekly study based on their sermons. The main topic is recapped and laid out in simplistic fashion so that individuals or groups can utilize them for their own study.

201 Ice Breakers (McGraw Hill, 1997) or the *Big Book of Ice Breakers* (McGraw Hill, 1999), by Edie West. Both books are good for breaking down the barriers so that group members become more comfortable with each other.

40 Days of Community Campaign will motivate members to step outside of their holy huddles and become involved in care and compassion opportunities. Saddleback Church designed this resource to be used during a church-wide campaign, particularly in small groups, to move members into action in their community by doing service-oriented projects. Ideally churches should have already been through the *40 Days of Purpose Campaign* based on the *Purpose-Driven Life*. The seeds planted in the hearts of members during that unifying campaign will make it much easier to motivate them to use their God-given design in service for others. You'll find it at <http://www.purposedriven.com/en-US/40DayCampaigns/CampaignInitiativeListing.htm>.

General Ministry Resources. Resources for equipping and encouraging pastors, volunteers, and church leaders including but not limited to the following topics: spiritual gifts, volunteer equipping, leadership, small groups, and general ministry-related topics. Includes a free ministry e-zine <http://www.ministryinmotion.net>.

endnotes

Chapter 1

1. Paul Tournier, quoted in "Chapter 12: Loneliness," Gary R. Collins Web site, http://www
.garyrcollins.com/index.php?option=com_content&task=category&sectionid=1&id=9&Itemid=
33 (accessed October 5, 2007).

Chapter 2

1. Oak Brook Community Church, "Home Groups," Oakbrookchurch.net, http://oak
brookchurch.net/homegroups.html (accessed January 3, 2006).

2. Brenda Nixon, "Silence! Why Your Audience Won't Participate," *Christian Communicator*
(March 2002).

Chapter 3

1. Dan Chun, "A Blue Print for Small Groups," Old Man New Man, http://www.oldmannew
man.com (accessed October 5, 2007). Online article is a reprint that appeared in the March/
April 2001 issue of *New Man Magazine*.

2. Terry Whalin, Mount Hermon's Christian Writers Conference attended by author in April
2005. Used by permission.

Chapter 4

1. Todd Szymczak, "The Power of Small Groups," Youth Ministry Exchange, http://
www.ymexchange.com/Youth-Ministry-Articles/The-Power-of-Small-Groups.html (accessed October 5, 2007).

2. Laurie Beth Jones, *Jesus CEO* (New York: Hyperion, 1995), 122.

3. Story appeared originally as "A Small Group Connection," by Teena Stewart, in *MIM
Ezine* (November 2002), http://www.ministryinmotion.net (article no longer online).

4. For more information about doing a Connection, see Steve Gladen and Brett Eastman,
Small Group Connection Kit, available through Small Group Ministries, http://www.smallgroups
.net/catalog.asp?SectionID=3&SubSection=2&HeadID=13 (accessed October 30, 2007).

Chapter 5

1. Patrick Morley, "How to Lead a Weekly Men's Small Group," Man in the Mirror,
http://www.maninthemirror.org/alm/alm94.htm (accessed October 29, 2007). Reprinted with
permission © Patrick Morley, Ph.D., Chairman and CEO of Man in the Mirror, Inc.

2. Jeff Van Vonderen, *Good News for the Chemically Dependent and Those Who Love Them*
(Minneapolis: Bethany House, 2004).

3. Ibid., 221

Chapter 6

1. Brett Eastman, "The Movement to Change Society," ChristianityToday.com, http://www
.christianitytoday.com/smallgroups/articles/movement.html (accessed October 5, 2007).

Chapter 7

1. Dale Galloway, quoted in "Developing and Using Small Groups," by Linda Hardin,
www.mccsf.org/worship/special/Developing%20and%20Using%20Small%20Groups.doc (accessed October 5, 2007).

2. Tim Burns, interview by author, April 12, 2005.

3. Lisa Beamer, interview by author, April 4, 2005.

4. Charles Caleb Colton, Quotes and Poem.com, http://www.quotesandpoem.com/quotes/showquotes/author/charles-caleb-colton/22110 (accessed October 5, 2007).

5. Dwight L. Moody, "Dwight L. Moody Quotes," BrainyQuote, http://www.brainy quote.com/quotes/authors/d/dwight_l_moody.html (accessed October 5, 2007).

Chapter 8

1. John Eldredge, *Waking the Dead: The Glory of a Heart Fully Alive* (Nashville: Thomas Nelson, 2003), 202.

Chapter 9

1. Henry Cloud, *Small Groups Conference 2004: Dealing with Problems in Groups* (Barrington, Ill.: Willow Creek Association, 2004), audiocassette, September 30—October 2, 2004.

2. Rick Warren, Purpose Driven Conference attended by author in May 2002.

Chapter 10

1. Bob Muni, "Will We Get the Message," The Forerunner, http://forerunner.com/fore runner/X0625_Will_We_Get_the_Mess.html (accessed October 5, 2007).

Chapter 11

1. Michael Moynagh, *emergingchurch.intro* (Oxford: Monarch Books, 2004), 10.

2. Ibid., 59-75.

3. Reggie McNeal, *The Present Future* (San Francisco: Jossey-Bass, 2003), 42.

4. Warren, Purpose Driven Conference.

Chapter 12

1. Morley, "How to Lead a Weekly Men's Small Group." Reprinted with permission © Patrick Morley, Ph.D., Chairman and CEO of Man in the Mirror, Inc.

Chapter 13

1. Oscar Wilde, "Oscar Wilde Quotes," BrainyQuote, http://www.brainyquote.com/quotes/authors/o/oscar_wilde.html (accessed October 5, 2007).

2. Story appeared originally as "Welcome to the Cholesterol Café," by Teena Stewart, in *MIM Ezine* (October 2004), http://www.ministryinmotion.net/MIMOct_3_2004.html (accessed October 19, 2007).

3. Sing the Faith Series (Minneapolis: Augsburg Fortress, 2002-3).

4. Lisa Beamer, interview.

Chapter 14

1. Kevin Robertson, "Coach's Corner," *Building Healthy Small Groups* 2, no. 1, (March 2004) http://www.saddlebackfamily.com/membership/images/mvsg_news0304.pdf (accessed October 5, 2007). Used by permission.

Chapter 15

1. Monique Woodward, http://www.interisland.net/woodward (accessed Sept 9, 2005). Used by permission.

2. Ministry Tools Resource Center, "Body Life in the Christian Church Community: Relating to One Another—The One Another Commands in Scripture," 1999—2005, http://mintools.com/bodylife4.htm (accessed August 30, 2007).